Robert McCloskey

Twayne's United States Author Series
Children's Literature

Ruth K. MacDonald, Editor
Purdue University Calument

TUSAS 558

Robert McCloskey, 1940 or 1941
*Reproduced by permission of Robert McCloskey and the May Massee
Collection, Emporia State University, Emporia, Kansas.*

Robert McCloskey

By Gary D. Schmidt

Calvin College

Twayne Publishers • Boston
A Division of G.K. Hall & Co.

Robert McCloskey
Gary D. Schmidt

Copyright © 1990 by G. K. Hall & Co.
All rights reserved.
Published by Twayne Publishers
A Division of G. K. Hall & Co.
70 Lincoln Street
Boston, Massachusetts 02111

Copyediting supervised by Barbara Sutton
Book production by Gabrielle B. McDonald

Typeset in 10/13 Century Schoolbook
by Compset, Inc., of Beverly, Massachusetts

Printed on permanent/durable acid-free paper
and bound in the United States of America

First published 1990
10 9 8 7 6 5 4 3 2 1

Library of Congress Cataloging-in-Publication Data

Schmidt, Gary D.
      Robert McCloskey/Gary D. Schmidt.
           p.   cm. — (Twayne's United States authors series; TUSAS
      558. Children's literature)
      Includes bibliographical references.
      ISBN 0-8057-7546-3 (alk. paper)
      1. McCloskey, Robert, 1914–   —Criticism and interpretation.
      2. Children's stories, American—History and criticism.   I. Title.
      II. Series: Twayne's United States authors series; TUSAS 558.
      III. Series: Twayne's United States authors series. Children's
      literature.
      PS3563.C3416Z87   1990   89-39850
      813'.54—dc20   CIP

For
Gertrude Allison Smith
and
Frederick Austin Stickney

Contents

Preface

Drawing a tree, you would think of the relationship
and proportions of twigs to branches to trunk, even
of the roots that you do not see. And you must feel
the balance and thrust of this growing thing, and its
relationship to other trees, a rock, the ocean. Your
hand is trained, of course, and it obediently moves a
pencil or brush across the page. But your mind is
ticking away like mad, racing and comparing and
thinking a thousand things that no one will ever see
in the picture. But the picture will be different for
your having thought of them.[1]

This is a book about seeing. A recurrent theme in Robert
McCloskey's interviews and speeches is the necessity for seeing.
Rejecting technological reductionism, McCloskey argues that the
ability to see clearly, to perceive accurately, is just as important
as learning to read and write. "I think what I feel is lacking is the
ability to look at something and evaluate it and know what you're
seeing. . . . [Most people have] never really looked at a tree . . . it's
just such a simple, basic thing, not bothering to look."[2]

This study argues that the process of "bothering to look" inevi-
tably links McCloskey's prose to his art; to speak of him simply
as an illustrator or as an author is to negate a fundamental assumption of his work in children's literature: visual perception is
as crucial to the effect of a story as is textual perception. That
McCloskey's principal subject matter is the world directly around
him is evidence of his claim that a person's immediate experience
can be a time of wonder—if the person bothers to look.

McCloskey himself has suggested that the artist spends fifty
weeks getting ready for the lightning strikes, and about two
weeks being creative. "You spend an awful lot of your time absorbing," he notes. "All the creative part is done in the first hour,

hour and a half." The rest of the time is involved in simply getting the idea down and giving it shape.[3] It is difficult to define the springs of creativity; perhaps after John Bunyan's opening claim in *Pilgrim's Progress*—"I dreamed, and, behold, I saw"—there is little more to say about creativity. But what can be examined is the "time absorbing." And this study suggests that McCloskey found in his own life the materials for story.

This does not mean that McCloskey simply recounted actual events with no mediation. Like trees seen in relationship to other trees, a rock, the ocean, these stories are mediated through the artist's eye, and they are transformed according to the exigencies of the story and its meaning. The Soldiers and Sailors Monument in *Lentil*, Homer's bedroom in *Homer Price,* Swain's Cove in *One Morning in Maine,* the rock on the point of the island in *Time of Wonder*—all are recast through the artist's imagination to become part of a tale and to impart their own appropriate meanings.

Hence the geographical organization of this study. In his own work McCloskey moved from the Midwest, to Boston, to the coast of Maine. Though his collaborative work ranged from nineteenth-century California to the mountains of Appalachia, his "time absorbing" came principally from these three areas. Their archetypal nature has led to McCloskey's being identified as a writer and illustrator of American life, but perhaps it would be more accurate to say that he is a writer and illustrator of the child's life. His perception of the nature of that child's life and his use of geography in its interpretation are two of the areas examined in this text.

What has not been examined in depth is the last two decades of Robert McCloskey's life, during which he has not been working as a writer. McCloskey himself has been reticent about these years, and this writer has chosen not to pry into them but instead to examine principally the years when McCloskey was producing children's literature.

I have chosen to use reproductions from those McCloskey texts that are printed in only one color. To reproduce an illustration from *Journey Cake, Ho!* or *Time of Wonder* or *Burt Dow* in a black-and-white format belies the author's intent, and the reader is respectfully directed to the primary texts themselves.

In the course of writing this book, I traveled east with my family to visit McCloskey. He brought us out to his island, and we spent an afternoon exploring, skipping rocks, and watching the clouds cross the bay. I suspect that my children, the oldest not yet four, will only remember fleeting glimpses of that time. What they do remember will be linked to images in *One Morning in Maine* and *Time of Wonder*. What I will remember is sitting on the veranda, talking with McCloskey about his books, watching the time of the world go by across Penobscot Bay, and listening to my children rearrange the coastline as they thudded rocks into the calm water. This, too, was a "time absorbing."

Gary D. Schmidt

Calvin College, Grand Rapids, Michigan

Acknowledgments

The genre of this sort of thing generally calls for a concluding kudo to one's spouse, but I wish to assert here, at the beginning, the tremendous debt I owe to my wife. Her critical acumen, her writing skills, and her love and understanding of McCloskey's work have contributed enormously to whatever is of any value in this study. And these things were, in some ways, merely the least of what she gave.

I also wish to thank Robert McCloskey himself, who invited my family to his island for a spectacular summer afternoon. His willingness to recall his career and to discuss his books has proven invaluable to this writer. My thanks also to Keith Robertson, Marc Simont, and Morton Schindel for their willingness to contribute to this study.

This study owes a debt to a number of librarians in North American collections. I particularly wish to thank Consuelo W. Harris of the Public Library of Cincinnati and Hamilton County; Adrienne M. Jenness of the Free Library of Philadelphia; Jill Shefrin of the Osborne Collection of Early Children's Books, Toronto Public Library; Ron Brown and Diane Farrell of the Boston Public Library; Lynne Hopkins of Calvin College Library, Grand Rapids; and Col. Charles W. McClain, Jr., and Jean Marie Ward of the Department of Defense Information, the Pentagon. I wish especially to thank Conrad Bult of Calvin College Library, who tracked down innumerable small leads with the skill, efficiency, and grace that are his alone.

A great debt is owed to Mary E. Bogan, curator of the May Massee Collection at Emporia State University, Emporia, Kansas. The time I spent with her working in that collection were some of the most profitable days of research I have ever spent, and I thank her for her many kindnesses and for the efficiency with

which she oversees that collection. My thanks also to Joyce Red-
ding, lecturer, and to the student assistants who worked so dili-
gently with me during my stay in Kansas: Melissa Frakes,
Michael Knecht, Lia McDowell.

This study was aided by a Calvin College Research Fellowship
and a Calvin College Alumni Association Faculty Research
Grant. The fact that it was converted from scribblings on legal
pads to the green electricity of a word processor is due principally
to Alma Walhout, Keri Bruggink, and Kathy Struck, all of Calvin
College.

The following items are cited or quoted from by permission of
the May Massee Collection and Elizabeth Fitton Folin: letter from
May Massee to Bertha Miller, 2 July 1943; letter from May Massee to Bertha Miller, 23 September 1943; letter from May Massee
to Bertha Miller, 24 September 1943; letter from May Massee to
Bertha Miller, 11 October 1943.

The following items are quoted from by permission of the author: letter from Marc Simont to Gary Schmidt, 21 March 1988;
letter from Keith Robertson to Gary Schmidt, 13 July 1987.

The following item is quoted from by permission of Morton
Schindel: *Robert McCloskey*. Dr. Morton Schindel. Weston Woods.
1964.

The following item is quoted from by permission of Morton
Schindel and the May Massee Collection: interview of May Massee by Morton Schindel, 1962.

The following item is quoted from by permission of Margaret
McCloskey, David Durand, and the May Massee Collection: letter
from Ruth Sawyer to Jessie Orton Jones and Elizabeth Orton
Jones, October 1943.

The following item is quoted from by permission of Charles M.
Daugherty and the May Massee Collection: letter from James
Daugherty to May Massee, 27 September 1943.

The following items are cited or quoted from by permission of
Robert McCloskey and the May Massee Collection: references to
the sketchbooks for *Homer Price,* including references to a model
for Homer and fallen trees drawn in Alabama; reference to an
early sketch for the cover of *Centerburg Tales,* where the book is

entitled *Centerburg Stories*; quotes from drafts for the opening of *Centerburg Tales* and "Experiment 13"; reference to an unused drawing for *The Man Who Lost His Head;* references to and quotes from the original dummy for *Make Way for Ducklings*; reference to a piece of experimental art work in color of the Public Garden, not used in *Make Way For Ducklings*; references to the sketchbooks for *Blueberries for Sal*; references to and quotes from a dummy for *Blueberries for Sal*; quotes from a dummy for *One Morning in Maine*; reference to a quote from Bert Dow giving permission for the use of his name, preserved on the back of a sketch of Bert Dow by Robert McCloskey; references to and quotes from a dummy for *Burt Dow*; "The Creative Process: A May Massee Workshop." Emporia, Kansas: Emporia State University, 20 June 1973; "The May Massee Workshop on Oral History." Emporia, Kansas: Emporia State University, 1 August 1983.

The following item is quoted from by permission of the Viking Press, Inc., and the May Massee Collection: letter from Morris Colman to Robert McCloskey, 2 August 1957.

The following items refer to quotations from texts by Robert McCloskey, Ruth Sawyer, and Claire Bishop:

From *Blueberries for Sal* by Robert McCloskey. Copyright 1948, renewed © 1976 by Robert McCloskey. All rights reserved. Reprinted by permission of Viking Penguin, a division of Penguin Books USA, Inc.

From *Burt Dow: Deep-Water Man* by Robert McCloskey. © 1963 by Robert McCloskey. All rights reserved. Reprinted by permission of Viking Penguin, a division of Penguin Books USA, Inc.

From *Lentil* by Robert McCloskey. Copyright 1948, renewed © 1968 by Robert McCloskey. All rights reserved. Reprinted by permission of Viking Penguin, a division of Penguin Books USA, Inc.

From *Make Way for Ducklings* by Robert McCloskey. Copyright 1941, renewed © 1969 by Robert McCloskey. All rights reserved. Reprinted by permission of Viking Penguin, a division of Penguin Books USA, Inc.

From *One Morning in Maine* by Robert McCloskey. Copyright 1952, renewed © 1980 by Robert McCloskey. All rights reserved. Reprinted by permission of Viking Penguin, a division of Penguin Books USA, Inc.

This study is dedicated to Gertrude Allison Smith and Frederick Austin Stickney, who now wait with joy for joy.

Chronology

1914 John Robert McCloskey born in Hamilton, Ohio, 15 September, to Howard Hill and Mable (Wismeyer) McCloskey.

1932 *George Washington Bicentennial Calendar* published for American History Club of Hamilton High School. Begins three years of study at the Vesper George School of Art, Boston. May Massee, McCloskey's future editor, leaves Doubleday to become editor of Junior Books at Viking Press.

1934 Receives commission for the sculptures for Hamilton municipal building.

1935 Meets May Massee and is told to go and learn how to draw. Receives a commission for a new cover for *Trigger John's Son*.

1936 Begins study at the National Academy of Design, New York. Awarded the National Academy's President's Award.

1938 After returning from Ohio, shows a draft of *Lentil* to May Massee; the book is accepted. Accepts commission for the Francis Scott Bradford mural.

1939 Moves to Greenwich Village, New York, and begins work on *Make Way for Ducklings*. Wins Prix de Rome. Awarded the Tiffany Foundation Prize.

1940 *Lentil*. Marries Margaret Durand, 23 November.

1941 *Make Way for Ducklings*. Illustrates Anne Malcolmson's *Yankee Doodle's Cousins*.

1942 Illustrates Robert Davis's *Tree Toad*. Illustrates Claire Huchet Bishop's *The Man Who Lost His Head*. Receives his first Caldecott Award for *Make Way for Ducklings*.

1943 *Homer Price.* Enters the Army, stationed at Fort Mc-Clellan, Alabama, for the next three years.

1945 Daughter Sarah (Sally) born, Ithaca, New York. Moves family to a chain of islands in Penobscot Bay, Maine.

1948 *Blueberries for Sal.* Daughter Jane born. Begins a year of study at the American Academy, Rome.

1949 Illustrates Tom Robinson's *Trigger John's Son.*

1951 *Centerburg Tales.*

1952 *One Morning in Maine.*

1953 Illustrates Ruth Sawyer's *Journey Cake, Ho!*

1955 Illustrates Anne White's *Junket, The Dog Who Liked Everything "Just So."* Weston Woods films *Make Way for Ducklings.*

1956 Weston Woods films *Lentil.*

1957 *Time of Wonder.*

1958 Illustrates Keith Robertson's *Henry Reed, Inc.* Receives his second Caldecott Award for *Time of Wonder.*

1960 May Massee retires from Viking Press and becomes an advisory editor.

1961 Weston Woods films *Time of Wonder.*

1963 *Burt Dow: Deep-Water Man.* Illustrates *Henry Reed's Journey.*

1964 Weston Woods films *The Doughnuts.* Honorary Doctor of Literature degree, Miami University, Oxford, Ohio.

1966 Illustrates *Henry Reed's Baby-Sitting Service.* May Massee dies, Christmas Eve.

1967 Weston Woods films *Blueberries for Sal.* Doctor of Letters degree, Mount Holyoke College, South Hadley, Massachusetts. The May Massee Memorial Committee founded.

1970 Illustrates *Henry Reed's Big Show.*

1971 Participates in Purdue University's "Old Masters" program.

1972 The May Massee Collection established at Emporia State University, Emporia, Kansas.

1974 Awarded the Regina Medal by the Catholic Library Association.

1976 Weston Woods films *The Case of the Cosmic Comic.*

1983 Weston Woods films *Burt Dow: Deep-Water Man.*

1987 Nancy Schon's bronze sculptures of the Mallard family placed in the Boston Public Garden.

1

"When You Learn to Play the Harmonica"

On 4 June 1959 the American Institute of Graphic Arts presented the first of its annual medals to May Massee, children's book editor at Viking Press. Its inscription read "Her Guidance Awakens Inspiration." Arguably the most important editor of children's books in the twentieth century, Massee had been guiding authors and artists for three decades at Viking Press, collecting a stable of writers that included Newbery Award–winning authors Ruth Sawyer, Kate Seredy, and James Daugherty; Caldecott Medal winners Robert McCloskey and Ludwig Bemelmans; and Newbery and Caldecott Award–winning Robert Lawson.

In accepting the award Massee reflected on her own sudden awareness as a child that she was forever to be incapable of drawing.

> I was very sorry for that child at that point but I am not sorry now because ever since then the law of compensation has been working for her. I know now that an artist must have a seeing eye but he must also have seeing hands. I had the seeing eye but not the seeing hands. I never lost my love of drawings—that grew with the years—and with it came understanding and appreciation of what artists can do.[1]

In defining the artist here Massee was too exclusive. While looking back on his career, one of Massee's most prominent artists,
Robert McCloskey, deprecated the use of hands for the artist.
"True, hands do play a part in drawing, but it's an automatic part,
like shuffling cards or knitting. Drawing is most of all a way of
seeing or of thinking."[2] The story of Robert McCloskey is in fact
the story of the search for "a way of seeing or of thinking," a way
of re-creating the world through the vision of the artist. And it is
the story of May Massee's contribution to that vision.

McCloskey's early years were at once the time of his search to
train his hands and also the time when a vision of the world was
being formed. Born 15 September 1914, in Hamilton, Ohio,
McCloskey spent his childhood in the Midwest, a setting he would
re-create in three of his books. Hamilton of the 1920s and 1930s
was a manufacturing town, set on the banks of the Great Miami
River. Its heavy industry included paper and pulp mills, foun-
dries, and machine tool factories. The McCloskey family lived
away from the industrial center, in a modest home on a suburban
street.

Stuart Fitton, a close friend of the artist as he was growing up
and later the family lawyer, remembers McCloskey's father as
being tall and gangly, contemplative, and an ingenious inventor.
Fitton recalls McCloskey's mother as being reserved and quiet.[3]
The son inherited his father's interest in machines, as well as his
mother's interest in painting. He himself would later note that
his parents "were very sympathetic to me, provided me with
brushes and paints and crayons."[4]

McCloskey attended Hamilton's public schools and began to
conceive of himself as a musician. "From the time my fingers were
long enough to play the scale, I took piano lessons."[5] He also
learned to play the drums and the oboe, as well as the harmonica.
After organizing a harmonica band, McCloskey toured local
grange meetings and lodges. His first character, Lentil, would be
a harmonica player, and many years later McCloskey would take
Lentil's place, playing a harmonica in a bathtub while hosting
American Songfest, a Weston Woods film.

Music was not his only expression of art, his only training of the hands; he also thought that he might wish to be an engineer. "I collected old electric motors and bits of wire, old clocks, and Meccano sets. I built trains and cranes with remote controls, my family's Christmas trees revolved, lights flashed and buzzers buzzed, fuses blew and sparks flew."[6] McCloskey has several times identified his own childhood with the "comfortable clutter" of Homer Price's world, but his mechanical interest figures in many of his works, including *Blueberries for Sal, One Morning in Maine, Burt Dow,* and the Henry Reed series. Since his last picture book, McCloskey has returned to this interest, so that his studio is more a machine shop than anything else.

Though these two interests—music and engineering—would continue, McCloskey would eventually choose a third option: the creation of art through drawing. He had always shown interest in art, but this first manifested itself through sculpture. During his high school years he taught a YMCA class in airplane modeling and another in soap sculpture. At the Hamilton YMCA he carved a totem pole. "I was carving larger and larger things, from bars of soap to trunks of trees."[7] The totem pole eventually led to a commission to produce sculpture for a new municipal building in Hamilton, and in six months, McCloskey, now nineteen, finished medallions illustrating Hamilton's industries and arts, twenty bas-reliefs, and several cast aluminum pieces.[8]

But McCloskey was also drawing. He began illustrating the Hamilton High School annual, and in 1932 the American history club of Hamilton High School published his first illustrated book, *George Washington Bicentennial Calendar.* In that same year he accepted a scholarship to the Vesper George School of Art in Boston, where he was to study for three winters, counseling at a boys' camp near Hamilton during the summers. (It was during this period—1934—that he received the commission for the Hamilton municipal building.) McCloskey was later to suggest that "my own life as a child in Ohio ended when I came east to art school."[9]

When the art director of Houghton Mifflin saw some of his paintings on exhibition, he asked McCloskey to come to his offices to see him. Though McCloskey was eventually to illustrate one book for Houghton Mifflin—Anne Malcolmson's *Yankee Doodle's*

Cousins (1941)—nothing further came of that meeting. In 1935, however, while on spring break from art school, McCloskey traveled to New York with some friends. He planned to visit May Massee; Stuart Fitton, his boyhood friend in Hamilton, was her nephew, so she was a logical beginning point for an artist who was becoming interested in children's books.

> I remember it was a rainy day and my first time in New York, and . . . I was going to find her office on 48th Street and, of course, I got East and West 48th Street mixed up. I was on the wrong side of Fifth Avenue and getting wetter and wetter and my folio wetter and wetter, and I finally got that straightened out. I found Viking Press and crept in there, dripping water, with my portfolio. And she looked me over; she was a wonderful woman. I remember coming into her office all wet, and she made me feel at home.[10]

McCloskey showed Massee his work, but she did not show immediate enthusiasm.

> She looked at the examples of "great art" that I had brought along (they were woodcuts, fraught with black drama). I don't remember just the words she used to tell me to get wise to myself and to shelve the dragons, Pegasus, and limpid pool business, and learn how and what to "art" with. I think we talked mostly of Ohio.[11]

Nevertheless, Massee did give McCloskey his first commission in children's literature: to create a new book jacket for Tom Robinson's *Trigger John's Son*. And later that night, she took him to dinner at the Cosmopolitan Club.

> Here I am a little wet child from Boston, and I meet up with a real editor from a publisher and I'm taken to dinner in . . . one of "the" clubs in New York. I remember to this day that she got me a cocktail before dinner and I was so impressed.[12]

Deciding to take Massee's advice, McCloskey moved to New York to learn how to draw. He spent two years at the National Academy of Design, in the summers painting at Provincetown, on the tip of Cape Cod. He achieved some success here; at the Academy he exhibited his work and was given the President's Award. His paintings were also exhibited at the Society of Independent Artists in Boston and at the Tiffany Foundation. Nevertheless, he recalls, "I never sold an oil painting, only a few watercolors at the most modest prices, and financially my art career was a bust."[13] McCloskey did some commercial work on such things as cartoon strips. Eventually he realized that though such work might be profitable, he was not developing as an artist. And so he returned to Ohio, where he painted the things he saw about him and began work on *Lentil*.

McCloskey went back to see May Massee in 1938. Twenty-five years later, she recalled this visit.

> One day, a young man came in with some of his work, and it was a dummy of *Lentil*. And I looked at it and was crazy about it. . . . And he said, "You like it?" I said, "Yes, I like it very much." He said, "You're really going to publish it?" "Yes," I said, "we're really going to publish it. . . ." He sat back in his chair. He said, "Miss Massee, you wouldn't remember, but I was here three years ago with my work, and you told me to go home and learn how to draw. And so I did." He didn't say a word to me. He went home and learned how to draw.
>
> And he has been our absolutely best person ever since.[14]

Nevertheless, there was some significant work to do on *Lentil*. McCloskey's original story was enormously long, and Massee suggested that it be drastically cut. McCloskey worked on the drawings for over a year, again receiving suggestions from Massee. He had wanted to bleed the illustrations off the page, but Massee resisted this. In fact, she resisted this practice until *Time of Wonder,* when McCloskey asked her to look at the illustrations in three dimensions.[15] *Lentil* was finally published in 1940.

In the same week that he signed his contract for *Lentil*, Mc-Closkey accepted a commission for a mural, won through new paintings he had worked on in Ohio. He moved to Boston to assist Francis Scott Bradford in painting a work illustrating the famous people who had lived on Beacon Hill. The other assistant was Marc Simont, and together they had a studio on Otis Place, a small street not far from Beacon Hill. The three painted several murals for Lever Brothers, designed to be a memorial to the head of that company as he was about to retire. However, upon his retirement, the building was sold to the Massachusetts Institute of Technology and the paintings are now housed in the Faculty Club on Memorial Drive.

McCloskey's next project was to become his most popular book, *Make Way for Ducklings*. Conceived during his walks to and from art school in Boston, *Make Way for Ducklings* represented the maturing of McCloskey's art, particularly in terms of the union of visual and textual narrative. The concept of the story itself took four years to develop; the drawings took additional years of study, involving hundreds of sketches of Boston, of ducks, of characters. It was published in 1941.

Make Way for Ducklings was to garner McCloskey his first Caldecott Medal. Later he wondered if Massee had held up the publication of the book to make sure that none of the other books coming out on her list rivaled it.[16] This may have been the case, for in the three years prior to *Make Way for Ducklings*, Viking published James Daugherty's *Andy and the Lion* (1938) and Ludwig Bemelman's *Madeline* (1939), both winners of Caldecott honors, and Robert Lawson's *They Were Strong and Good* (1940), a Caldecott winner. McCloskey himself was unaware of the award. "I had to say, 'What's that?' when May called up and said, 'You won it!' I didn't know from anything what it was."[17]

In the years directly after *Make Way for Ducklings* McCloskey illustrated for two other publishers: Houghton Mifflin published his illustrated *Yankee Doodle's Cousins* (1941) and Lippincott published *Tree Toad* (1942). Years later McCloskey recalled,

> I knew she [May Massee] wasn't happy about them after they would come out, but I think she thought, "Well, he'll

learn." And I did because . . . I expected all of them to be as well produced, as well thought out as books that came out of Viking Press. And when I found out that [the book] didn't look anything like the book I had imagined . . . well, so you learn.[18]

Perhaps McCloskey's judgment is somewhat unfair, considering that these books were published during the war years when many publishers were forced to cut back on some of their quality. In any event, they were the last books that McCloskey was to illustrate for any publisher other than Viking.

In the same month that he signed the *Lentil* contract, he met Margaret Durand, the daughter of the Newbery Award winner Ruth Sawyer. They would marry in 1940, and McCloskey used her as a model first as the librarian in *Homer Price* (she was in fact a children's librarian when they met) and later in the Maine books. "I used her as a model for *Blueberries for Sal*," he recalls, "but she wasn't very cooperative when I was doing that book. She was pregnant with Jane at the time and pretty cranky about it."[19]

Soon after the publication of *Make Way for Ducklings* the United States entered World War II. With *Lentil* and *Make Way for Ducklings* McCloskey had come to be identified as an author of Americana. Actually he was participating in a kind of nation-alized artistic movement. He recalls,

> in the thirties in the Depression days, Americana was the big theme of American art; we were just beginning to discover ourselves. . . . [T]here was a lot of Americana in all the art; we were very saturated with it back in those days. . . . We were sort of tossing out a lot of arti-ness that had come over from abroad, and I think that a lot of this feeling came naturally, and some of it I ac-quired; the two are inseparable in some ways.[20]

It seems likely that McCloskey's movement toward Americana be-gan after his first meeting with May Massee; certainly *Lentil* is a product of his turning his thoughts away from high drama in art to the simplicity and innocence of the small midwestern town. But for contemporary reviewers *Homer Price* was his most American work, and it came out in the middle of the war—October 1943. For most reviewers, Homer was the archetypal American boy, representing all that was good in the American spirit.

Homer Price represented something of a change in McCloskey's career. All of his other works had been picture books; here for the first time he was predominantly dependent upon the text. This change was instigated by May Massee, who told McCloskey, "I haven't anything for you to illustrate, and why don't you go home and write something?"[21] For Massee, a project began with story. Speaking of the nature of picture books, McCloskey has noted that "May Massee said you must begin with a story, and the illustrations must add to and carry the story on, from page to page, but to her the text was the most important part of the book—'I know you can do the pictures,' she always said . . . 'but the text must still come first.'"[22] This emphasis on text led to works such as *Homer Price* and *Centerburg Tales*. It also led to longer texts for the picture books; none of the books written after *Homer Price* would have as simple and concise a text as either *Lentil* or *Make Way for Ducklings*.

McCloskey had wished to finish *Homer Price* before he went into the army, and though most of the book was completed, he did need to supply one additional illustration during the production process: the well-known error, where he drew five crooks instead of the four suggested by the text. He used himself as the principal model for Homer, though one rough sketch of a young boy holding a child suggests that there was at least one other model. By the sketch, McCloskey has noted

> Boy name of Weber
> Model for Homer
> Bucks County, PA
> About 1941–42[23]

Webber's facial features are sketched in only roughly, and the pose of the sketch is not used in *Homer Price,* though Homer does appear with Freddy's younger brother Louis.

In November 1943 *Horn Book* ran an unprecedented short article on *Homer Price.* Instead of reviewing the book with other books in its appropriate section, Bertha Miller, then editor of *Horn Book,* included a three-page comment on the book by Eric Gugler and James Daugherty. Both pieces included in this comment were commissioned by May Massee; the fact that Massee screened the reviews suggests her prestige and position in the field of children's literature. Miller had originally planned to ask Walter Brooks, writer of the *Freddy the Pig* series, to write the review, but Massee rejected this. "I like Walter Brooks and I like his books," she wrote to Miller, "but the older I get the more I realize authors just simply can't review each others' books, especially when they are in the same genre."[24] She went on to suggest Eric Gugler, the architect who designed her office at Viking Press. Miller agreed, and ten weeks later Massee wrote again: "Eric Gugler has written a perfectly killing letter about *Homer* but it will have to be fixed up more or less before you get it."[25]

Most of *Horn Book's* readership would not know Eric Gugler's name, so when James Daugherty saw May Massee the day after she had written enthusiastically to Miller about Gugler's comment, Massee wrote back to Miller: "Jimmy Daugherty was here yesterday. He was so keen about *Homer* that I asked him if he would take it and write me a letter about it. Then I thought I would put his and Eric Gugler's together as they would show two different points of view."[26] When Daugherty's letter came three weeks later, Massee wrote Miller once again: "I thought Jimmie's was a real review and Eric's showed the average man's instant response."[27]

Massee's observation was accurate: there are real distinctions between the two comments as they finally appeared, slightly edited, in *Horn Book.* Gugler's is a rambling piece, evoking scenes of childhood that *Homer Price* evoked for him. Daugherty spends some time on the genre of the book, but the bulk of his review deals with the illustrations. Both comments establish the archetypal Americanness of *Homer Price.* Daugherty began his letter to Massee by welcoming *Homer Price* "to Tom Sawyer's Gang, that immortal and formidable band of boys of American fiction." He wrote of its "American comic genius." "It is the true comedy of democracy in the great American tradition ... It is America laughing at itself with a broad and genial humanity, without bitterness or sourness or sophistication."[28]

Gugler saw Homer as the embodiment of all the childhood experiences of a typical American boy.

That turned-up nose and the freckles, the impudent, quizzical, honest little look reminds you of so many things. How much more than anything else in the world, even to be rich or powerful, even to be President, even to be anything ever so much more than anything else in the world, they [young boys] wanted to be able to whistle, very, very loud with two fingers stuffed in their mouths.

How you envied the boy with the perfect arrangement of teeth that made it possible for him to spit a thin jet of water in a high arched stream—the little duffer could make it land where he said it would.

No ambitions in later life will ever equal these, and you feel that Homer Price could do them all.[29]

McCloskey had not set out to write a novel of American youth; it was meant to be a collection of comic short stories set in the land of his own childhood, appropriate to his own childhood experiences. But in the middle of a war, in the middle of the time of identifying American values, for some *Homer Price* became a document stating what Americans were fighting for on the fields of Europe and the islands of the South Pacific.

Daugherty concluded his letter by noting that McCloskey had won a scholarship to study in Rome but had entered the army. "So if he is going to Rome," Daugherty wrote, "it will not be on the scholarship but to occupy it! . . . These young artists that we know who are in the army, how cheerfully and patiently and determinedly [sic] like all the rest they are going the grim job and how gladly and proudly we will welcome them back God willing, every one of them. And may the day be soon."[30] McCloskey had in fact entered the army before the publication of *Homer Price*. He was to spend three years at Fort McClellan, Alabama. "My greatest contribution to the war effort was inventing a machine to enable short second lieutenants to flip over large training charts in a high breeze," McCloskey noted.[31] He also illustrated charts depicting troop movements; with heavy use, these wore out quickly and none survive. At the same time he continued to sketch the things he saw around him. A number of these drawings survive, including two sketches of broken and fallen trees labeled "Alabama, 1945."[32] They strongly resemble the great fallen tree of *Time of Wonder.*

In October 1943, the same month that *Homer Price* was published, Ruth Sawyer wrote to Jessie and Elizabeth Orton Jones about McCloskey's army life: "Bob, poor dear, is at Fort McClellan, Alabama, the toughest of all camps. He writes he is keeping up better than 'most of the men of his age'—(28). And the most delightful news came when he wrote his sergeant cleaned for him his gun while he played the harmonica for the sergeant."[33] The story of the sergeant and his harmonica seems to have been a popular one; it was known by both May Massee and James Daugherty. McCloskey continued drawing training pictures, gaining the rank of sergeant. Upon his discharge in 1945 he headed to Maine.

He brought his family with him: Sally had been born in 1945. McCloskey's in-laws had spent a great deal of time in Maine, principally in Lincolnville. By the end of the war they were living in Hancock, farther up the coast. It was here that McCloskey and Peggy and Sally lived with them for the first month after his discharge. During that time the McCloskeys searched for a decommissioned lighthouse to purchase, but settled for a chain of three islands—one a six-acre island—in Penobscot Bay. "We came to this place cold," McCloskey recalls. "I don't know whether, looking back, I would have come out of the service, bought an island, and shot my wad trying to make it work. No one knew then that children's books would catch on as they did. I don't know if I would have had the courage to jump into it if I came into it a little later."[34]

They lived on the island for six months of the year; during the winter they lived in a number of different homes, one of which was a house owned by May Massee. To her, the McCloskeys were more than just tenants; soon May Massee virtually became part of their family. She had had a strong sense of family, and a desire to establish a home. And to this end she had asked Tom Robinson, an architect as well as a writer, to design a stone house for her. Built in Montgomery, New York, west of the Hudson River, it was constructed of stones and beams from old barns. There she hoped to gather her family around her. But she was not successful in this, and during the war she bought another house in Croton Falls, New York, east of the Hudson and more accessible from the city. It was here that the McCloskey family stayed, surrounded by Oriental rugs, textured wallpaper, and tapestries—evidence of May Massee's love of texture, which is also evident in the books published under her. There May Massee grew to know the Mc-Closkeys well.

Financially secure because of the royalties for *Make Way for Ducklings* that had been building up during the war, McCloskey began work on several new books. During this time Massee did not want him to work with other publishers, though she never indicated this in any kind of contractual agreement. Instead, she simply kept him busy. In 1947 Margaret McElderry, the children's book editor at Harcourt, Brace, sent McCloskey a manuscript about a boy who caught eels along the Hudson River. McCloskey was inclined to accept the commission, but soon after that he met with Massee, who asked him what he had begun.

By this time, McCloskey's first commission from Massee—the book jacket for *Trigger John's Son*—had languished for more than ten years. McCloskey had spoken to Massee about the need for illustrations throughout the text, and they had agreed that he would illustrate the new edition. They had also agreed that there was no need to press ahead with the project. But when McCloskey let Massee know of the McElderry offer, she asked, "Well, what about *Trigger John's Son*?" Soon after that, McCloskey turned down the offer from McElderry, who never again tried to get him to illustrate a Harcourt, Brace book.[35]

Blueberries for Sal, taken directly from the McCloskey family's experiences in Maine, was published in the fall of 1948. The book was inspired by the sounds that McCloskey recorded—"kuplink, kuplank, kuplunk"—as he sketched his wife and daughter picking blueberries on Little Deer Isle. The simplicity of its text recalls that of *Make Way for Ducklings,* but the carefully shaped sentence structures suggest McCloskey's growth as a writer as well as an artist. During the production process Viking Press had been concerned about the blueberry blue, but the final product pleased both editor and artist. The book was to garner McCloskey's first Caldecott Honor, behind that year's Caldecott Award winner, Berta and Elmer Hader's *The Big Snow.*

In 1948 Jane was born and the McCloskeys decided to winter on the island—the only time they did so. (When the bay froze over, McCloskey put runners on the dinghy to get back and forth to the mainland.) Soon after, the McCloskeys sailed to Italy, bringing with them the illustrations for *Trigger John's Son,* which McCloskey completed while in Rome. In 1939 he had won the Prix de Rome, but work on the manuscript of *Lentil* had delayed his acceptance. In any case, when war was declared in Europe, the other winners had been sent home. Now for a year McCloskey had a studio at the American Academy in Rome, where he was part of a beaux arts program, working with other artists in other fields. Principally he studied mosaic techniques, and one product of that study is a circular mosaic of a unicorn that now sits on the mantel in his island home. The techniques that he learned there did not particularly affect his children's books, and upon his return to Maine he took up new projects that were outgrowths of previous books.

The first of these projects was *Centerburg Tales,* another set of stories with Homer Price as the protagonist. Most of the stories are told by Grandpa Hercules, a narrator who is a teller of tall tales. The first four stories are his; the last three are closer to the tales of *Homer Price,* with Homer as a major participant. When McCloskey finished the stories and the book was about to go into publication, Massee decided that it needed one additional tale. She waited for a year while McCloskey wrote the last story, and the collection was finally published in 1951.

One Morning in Maine was published in April 1952. Reflecting the growing McCloskey family, the book was set on Scott Islands and along the coast of Penobscot Bay. Sal is older, about to lose her first tooth, and Jane is just a toddler. Their retriever Penny and cat Mozzarella are also participants in the tale. The book was to win McCloskey's second Caldecott Honor, behind Lynd Ward's *The Biggest Bear.*

Soon after work was completed on *One Morning in Maine,* McCloskey traveled to Mexico with his family, and his daughters were enrolled in school there. He had spent two months painting in Mexico in 1937, and when he went there again, he had a children's book in mind, though he was also beginning to feel that his art might start to move in directions other than children's picture books. He spent some time doing backgrounds for this book, but "it was an aborted project, like many others."[36] He returned to Maine and began work on *Journey Cake, Ho!* (1953), the book that would bring him his third Caldecott Honor behind Ludwig Bemelman's *Madeline's Rescue,* also published by Viking.

It was Ruth Sawyer's desire that McCloskey illustrate the book, and when Massee asked him, he agreed. For the first time in a picture book he created illustrations in several colors. It was, consequently, his first experience in making the color separations required for the printing process. The first edition was printed on a cream-colored paper that McCloskey chose, but Viking soon realized that it would be difficult to consistently find the same colored paper. "So they took white sheets of paper and ran them through the press one time, printing them all-over cream color before printing the book. . . . [Y]ou can see that process wouldn't last long in these days of conglomerates and cost-cutting."[37] Today the book is printed on paper that is almost white.

McCloskey was to collaborate on one additional book with Ruth Sawyer. When May Massee looked at it, she chose not to publish it. McCloskey refused to send it to another publisher and it was never published. The decision reflected McCloskey's commitment to May Massee and Viking Press, as well as his disappointments with other publishers.

After the publication of his next collaborative work—Anne H. White's *Junket*—McCloskey began concerted work on the text and drawings of *Time of Wonder.* By this time the McCloskey family had been living on the Penobscot Bay island for ten years, and McCloskey wanted to compress all of their summer experiences into a sixty-four-page book. He worked for three years on the book, creating illustrations that represented a markedly different style from those of his earlier books. It was his first published work in full color. Though he had wanted to use color earlier, Massee had resisted his suggestions, citing the enormous expense of producing such a book, as well as McCloskey's inexperience. In *Time of Wonder,* however, he worked with Massee's full encouragement, so that in his acceptance speech for the Caldecott Medal given to *Time of Wonder* he would suggest that in some ways this was May Massee's book. His acceptance marked the first time that any artist had won two Caldecott Medals, and, since then, only Chris Van Allsburg has duplicated that feat, winning two awards for books that the artist both wrote and illustrated.

Soon after *Time of Wonder* Massee asked McCloskey to illustrate Keith Robertson's *Henry Reed, Inc.,* and in 1958 that book was published. It was the first of four Henry Reed books that McCloskey was to illustrate, the last coming in 1970. By 1970 Viking Press had merged into a corporation, and McCloskey was becoming dissatisfied with the look of the books. In fact, *Henry Reed's Big Show* was the last book that he was to illustrate.

In 1960 May Massee retired from full-time work at Viking and became an advisory editor, working mostly out of her house at Croton Falls. It was here that McCloskey brought the dummy of *Burt Dow,* though this was not particularly unusual since he had sometimes read his stories to her when she came to the house while his family was living there. Like *Time of Wonder, Burt Dow* was to be published in full color. And both books were intimately tied to the experience of the McCloskey family in Maine.

Since *Make Way for Ducklings,* each of McCloskey's picture books had won a Caldecott Medal or a Caldecott Honor; *Burt Dow* won neither. The winner of the Caldecott Medal for 1963, the year *Burt Dow* was published, is significant in that it suggests that new trends were taking hold of children's literature in the early 1960s: Maurice Sendak's *Where the Wild Things Are.* Where

McCloskey had always pictured childhood as a time of exuberant joy and wonder, Sendak pictured it as a dangerous period, where the child was prey to destructive impulses, internal fears, and almost uncontrollable frustrations. Where McCloskey depicted the unity, strength, and love that comes from family, Sendak was to depict the child's alienation from the adult world. The two visions could not have been more different, and for at least the next two decades it would be Maurice Sendak's vision that would dominate children's literature.

McCloskey would not write another children's book after *Burt Dow*; instead, he turned to another medium: film. Under Morton Schindel, Weston Wood filmed four of McCloskey's books iconographically: *Make Way for Ducklings* (1955), *Lentil* (1956), *Time of Wonder* (1961), and *Blueberries for Sal* (1967). The first two films were among Weston Woods's earliest, where Schindel was just starting to use the iconographic method of filming. In this technique the illustrations are moved around a stationary camera, so that in the film, the camera seems to become the child's eye, moving from detail to detail. In 1983 Weston Woods filmed *Burt Dow: Deep-Water Man*. This film was animated, which meant the inclusion of hundreds of additional drawings that exactly matched McCloskey's original drawings for the picture book. It also meant the inclusion of several scenes not in the book to follow the text, such as a scene where Leela stands in front of the geranium-strewn rowboat to feed the chickens. McCloskey himself was very pleased with the final product; he continues to spend some time each year working with Weston Woods.

Weston Woods also produced two live-action films, both of stories from *Homer Price*. *The Doughnuts* was produced in 1964, the first live-action film based on a children's book to be produced in the United States. The film follows the text closely, the camera emphasizing the vast number of doughnuts through tracking shots and repeated shots of the doughnut machine. The film includes two "in" jokes: Homer refers to the telephone operator (unnamed in the book) as Miss Massee, and McCloskey himself appears as one of the customers who frenetically looks through a bag of doughnuts he has broken up to find the bracelet.

McCloskey also sold Weston Woods the rights to "Nothing New Under the Sun (Hardly)," and though Weston Woods got a car on which to build the mousetrap, they eventually chose to work on "The Case of the Cosmic Comic" instead. Produced in 1976, this film also follows the text closely, though it includes a black-and-white sequence depicting the film that Homer and his friends watch, parodying the super-hero films of the 1940s and 1950s. Morton Schindel himself is the stationmaster in the film.

Watching Morton Schindel animate his books interested McCloskey in animation and movement. As an outgrowth of that interest, he has been working to develop a new type of puppet since the mid-1960s. The principal goal of this project is to eliminate the strictures that bind puppets to small stages. So instead of being manipulated by strings held from above, these puppets are given movement through bound controlling rods handled from underneath, so that the puppet seems to move smoothly of its own accord, without apparent restriction. McCloskey sees these puppets as being used primarily in children's films.

Since the publication of *Burt Dow* McCloskey has received a number of awards and honors. In 1964 Miami University (Ohio) gave him an honorary doctor of literature degree. In 1967 Mount Holyoke College in South Hadley, Massachusetts, awarded McCloskey a doctor of letters degree. In 1971 he was part of Purdue's "Old Masters" program. In 1974 the Catholic Library Association awarded him its Regina Medal for his distinguished contributions to children's literature. And in the autumn of 1987 Nancy Schon's bronze depictions of the Mallard family were placed in the Boston Public Garden, an event that McCloskey and his wife attended.

In the mid-1970s McCloskey began work on a project designed to honor the editor who had done so much for his career. May Massee had died on Christmas Eve, 1966, after thirty years of service at Viking Press. A number of editors and authors who had known Massee and been influenced by her gathered to create some kind of memorial; the meetings were chaired by Keith Robertson. At McCloskey's suggestion, the memorial became a collection of materials by authors, artists, designers, typographers, and printers, all of whom had contributed to the production of Massee's books. The collection is now housed at Emporia State University, Emporia, Kansas, and it is here that most of McCloskey's original sketches and drawings are kept.

If it seems unlikely that the work of a New England artist be housed in a midwestern university, one need only consider the concluding observation of *Lentil*: "So you never can tell what will happen when you learn to play the harmonica."[38]

2

The Ohio Books:
The Myth of the Midwest

In placing three of his books in the Midwest McCloskey partici-
pated in a vision that saw the Midwest as a place of innocent
pleasure, delightful adventure, and small-town security. For
McCloskey, and other writers like William Saroyan who depicted
the life of a child in the 1940s, the geographic setting became a
metaphor for the state of childhood. In a world at war Alto and
Centerburg, perhaps unconsciously, set their own reality—the
imaginative life of a child—against another reality almost too
harsh to be borne.

George Washington Bicentennial Calendar

In 1932 McCloskey published the *George Washington Bicentennial Calendar,* a calendar and history, for the American History
Club of Hamilton High School. Each two-page spread of this small
pamphlet combines a page of text (compiled by the history teach-
ers of the school) describing a single aspect of Washington's career
with an appropriate scene, generally of a building. Only two illustrations of Washington himself appear, one a bust on the cover,
the other as he takes the presidential oath.

Early works are tempting things for critics, who seek in them
the signs of a master craftsman. But this is clearly the work of an

amateur artist, whose drawings lack artistic vision and instead are literal rather than interpretive representations of the world. McCloskey is confined by his material here. The illustration of Washington taking the oath of office seems literally drawn from one of the Federalist paintings. His woodcuts of Washington's birthplace, Mount Vernon, and Independence Hall suggest the stylized perspectives of a history text. (McCloskey would later transform similar elements, so that the formal lines of a stately house would be used for humorous effect in *Lentil* and *Homer Price.*)

But this is not to say that these pictures are crude things; an interest in line is evident. The title page strongly juxtaposes vertical lines—the columns of the Lincoln Memorial—and, seen through them, the Washington Monument. The diminishing perspective brings the eye to the base of the monument, whose black sharpness pierces the stark whiteness of the reflecting pool and the blank sky. In a similar way, the final woodcut uses vertical lines to connect the wrought-iron gate of Washington's tomb with cathedralic pillars above, suggesting an equation of those two settings. Conversely, his illustration of Valley Forge uses sinuous lines to suggest movement in the bare branches that surround one of the bunkhouses in the fort.

McCloskey's texturing of these illustrations looks forward to illustrations in some of his Maine picture books, though these were crafted in different media. The *George Washington Bicentennial Calendar* was executed in woodcuts, which McCloskey used to suggest the delicate softness of a flower garden, the crude outlines of a frontier outpost, the broad expanse of a sunset, the shadowed closeness of a furniture-stuffed room. His restraint in the use of color here also foreshadows the first two Maine books. The dominant color is a dark blue, printed on bone-white paper. Pink and light blue also appear, particularly as highlights in the skies.

Though for the most part these illustrations represent rigid, stilted poses (this mirrored in the diction of the text), a running story on the bottom of each page subverts the formality of both the prose and the illustrations. McCloskey includes the legendary cherry-tree incident here, the only part of the book that is not strict historical fact. A series of twelve silhouettes, one for each month, illustrates the tale. And here the characters are not rigid; they move in dramatically exaggerated postures. The backward leaning of the young Washington rushing off to test his new hatchet would be used later in *Journey Cake, Ho!* The exuberant motion of the actual chopping would be refined and used for more comic effect in *Homer Price* and *Centerburg Tales*. The silhouetted background would appear in *Blueberries for Sal*. These incidental drawings, rather than the pamphlet's principal illustrations, mark the routes that McCloskey would choose in his later picture books.

Lentil

It is generally the case that an accomplished author/illustrator begins with something of an apprenticeship, and only infrequently do the earliest books show evidence of the subsequent artistry and the expression of inner vision that becomes evident in the later work. It would have been difficult to predict that Barbara Cooney would win two Caldecott Awards from her first book, *Green Wagons* (1943), or that Maurice Sendak's *Atomics for the Millions* (1947) was the work of a future winner of the Hans Christian Andersen award.

But *Lentil* (1940) emerged without this apprenticeship, and it was all the more striking for that. Even today it does not have the appearance of a first book. Instead, it is a mature picture book representing a deep understanding not only of illustration, but of the relationship between illustration and text and how this relationship expresses meaning. And it is a work that announces many of the themes that McCloskey would deal with in later books, at the same time suggesting the literary and artistic approaches that he would take to those themes.

When McCloskey brought the original manuscript to May Massee, it was ponderously long and "read like a Thomas Wolfe novel," he recalls.[1] She suggested cuts and eventually it became a sixty-four-page picture book with a fairly short text, stripped of the Thomas Wolfe density and complex structure. Many pages have only a single sentence beside the illustration; some have only a fragment.

In the story Lentil is a young boy living in Alto, Ohio, who cannot sing or whistle; he sits abashed while his classmates sing from choir books and is scorned by birds when he cannot pucker his lips to whistle. He eventually buys a harmonica from a hardware store (the fact that it comes from a hardware store suggests the practical, no-nonsense feel of this midwestern town). He learns to play and delights all those that listen to him, except for Old Sneep, who does nothing but sit on a park bench, whittling and grumbling.

When the great Colonel Carter announces that he is coming back to Alto after a two-year absence, the entire town prepares a celebratory parade. Sneep is determined to thwart this parade, perhaps because of jealousy, or sheer meanness, or a sense of justice ("We wuz boys together . . . and he needs takin' down a peg or two," he claims).[2] Perched on top of the train station when Colonel Carter arrives, Sneep sucks on a lemon. When the band players hear him, their lips instantly pucker so that they cannot welcome the great colonel. Lentil, whose lips cannot pucker, begins to play "She'll Be Coming 'Round the Mountain" on his harmonica. At first annoyed, the colonel is soon entranced, and helps Lentil play as the town marches behind him to Colonel Carter's house, where he announces that he will fund the building of a new hospital.

Lentil is told in the partite structure that would characterize many of McCloskey's later works. In this structuring, it is the protagonist who unifies the book, rather than the progression of the plot. The plot itself is a collection of episodes, all using the same characters and setting, but all separate in terms of the plot situation. In *Lentil* McCloskey pairs two episodes that have separate movements to two distinct climaxes, but they are unified by a common means of resolution. Lentil solves his inability to sing by learning to play the harmonica; later he thwarts Sneep's malice by playing the same instrument. The harmonica has resolved both individual and communal difficulties.

This structure creates a form in which the episodes are separate and yet inextricably bound together; such a structure appears over and over again in McCloskey's work. He uses it to show the simultaneity of events in *Blueberries for Sal*. At other times it is used to establish a sequence of events, as in *One Morning in Maine*. In *Homer Price* the partite structure suggests the myriad events that go to make up childhood. And the structure is also used thematically to portray the inevitable passage of the seasons in *Time of Wonder*.

The structure also simulates the structure of a genre that McCloskey is always at least touching in *Lentil*: the tall tale. In several ways *Lentil* is a tall tale in the American tradition of tall tales. It uses the exaggerated characters of these tales (Sneep, Colonel Carter), the exaggerated situations (Sneep perched on top of the train station), the unruffled narrator who seems to be able to recount extraordinary events with no hint of surprise in his voice. The somewhat innocuous problem and the quick resolution are themselves the stuff of tall tales. Lentil himself stands apart from this genre; he is not Pecos Bill or John Henry or Stormalong. But as he witnesses the unfolding of the tall tale in his small town, Lentil takes on the stance of any reader who yearns to participate in the episodic adventures of those tales if only it were possible.

Lentil, like McCloskey's other picture books, is drawn from personal experience. Like Lentil, McCloskey played the harmonica and enjoyed practicing in the bathtub, where, the narrator of *Lentil* suggests, "the tone was improved one hundred per cent." Lentil's home town of Alto is much the same as Hamilton, and the landscape of the endpapers recalls the Ohio landscape of McCloskey's boyhood. The Soldiers and Sailors Monument is a scaled-down version of the one in Hamilton, and Colonel Carter's house is a recast version of one in Hamilton, though McCloskey has added a cupola and a stone wall rather than wrought iron fence. Lentil himself is a bit more rustic than McCloskey had been in his childhood, "though I wish I had been barefoot more of the time."[3] Even the unusual name Lentil came from McCloskey's past. A friend at the Vesper George Art School used to intone that "the pyramids were built on lentils," meaning that the slaves who built the pyramids ate lentils. Lentil's name really is a remnant from the first long draft of the manuscript, in which pyramids figured.[4]

But Lentil is not McCloskey, and Alto is not Hamilton; they are a character and a town re-created in the artist's imagination. (McCloskey did not go back to Hamilton while he was at work on *Lentil*; instead, he "remembered pictures.")[5] The result is that Alto became an imaginary midwestern small town with distinctive boundaries. The great Colonel Carter comes from the outside, but everyone else is part of Alto and the small-town world. It is an archetypal small town, with its parades, its typed townspeople, small park, Main Street, and infinite possibilities for an adventurous boy.

This bounded type of setting would appear over and over again in McCloskey's work: Homer Price's Centerburg, the island in Boston's Public Garden, Sal and Jane's island off the coast of Maine. Safe and secure worlds, they provide a context for the imaginative adventures of childhood while they insulate the characters from any real dangers. Nothing very bad happens in Alto— or in Boston or on the Maine coast. Instead, the world in each of McCloskey's books is a delightful place. The most simple yet wonderful moments of childhood adventures lie all about the characters.

Those adventures are wonderful principally because they occur in a simple context. The opening line—"In the town of Alto, Ohio, there lived a boy named Lentil"—is a simple declaration. Appropriately, it links Lentil and Alto, and both are uncomplicated, imaginative, and innocent. Lentil's great difficulty is hardly world-shaking: he simply cannot pucker his lips. And even that difficulty becomes an asset when it enables him to save the mayor's reputation and the goodwill of a powerful man at Colonel Carter's arrival. And this, in turn, leads to the funding and building of a hospital.

Even the world that Lentil inhabits is a simple one. Though he is often pictured on the edge of crowds, he does not participate in their activity by becoming part of that crowd. He is principally attended by animals: the dogs and cats of the back alleys, the squirrels of Carter Memorial Park. They are the ones who most closely observe both his inability to sing and his success with the harmonica. At the end of the book, however, this changes at his alliance with Colonel Carter. Together they play the harmonica, drive down Main Street, face the crowd from the front steps of the colonel's house, and essentially act as young boys, brought together through the medium of music.

This alliance raises the significance of McCloskey's opening stress on simplicity, for it is an alliance of the great with the small, of the renowned with the unknown, of the sophisticated with the rustic. And the ground they meet on is the ground of childhood; indeed, all of the townspeople meet here as they lick ice-cream cones on Colonel Carter's front porch. Through the alliance with Lentil, the lofty, Olympian colonel becomes a proper citizen of the simple town of Alto.

Lentil, like Homer Price, Trigger, Henry Reed, and, in some ways, Junket, is an observer of the adult world. Like Homer, Lentil is at times drawn into the conflicts of that world, but he is nonetheless apart from it. He is the child who witnesses the foibles of the adult world. And because he is the witness, the reader perceives that world through his eyes and with his perceptions. These perceptions, though simple and innocent, are accurate; his instinct to replace a brass band with a harmonica is the instinct of a child, but it is exactly right.

Old Sneep is the lone dissenting figure in the book, the one who refuses to participate in the general excitement of the town. He seeks to involve the reader in this discontent, looking directly at the reader and suggesting that his ill will is justified by the offensive pride of Colonel Carter. But because the reader is already looking through Lentil's eyes, and because Lentil himself is excited at the colonel's arrival, Sneep cannot make the reader into a confederate. This process is reversed at the end of the book when Lentil looks directly at the reader and establishes a sense of complicity.

Lentil's movement from the disharmony of his dreadful singing to the harmony of his harmonica is mirrored in Sneep's movement, for he too moves from disharmony to harmony. To interfere

with the arrival of the colonel, Sneep stations himself above the
rest of the town, thus placing himself literally in the position that
he suggests the colonel has taken metaphorically. That position
isolates him from the rest of the town as, in a sense, the colonel
has been separated from Alto. At the end, however, he too is eating an ice-cream cone in Colonel Carter's yard; his angry energy
expended, he rests on a cane. And McCloskey concludes that
"everybody was happy—even Old Sneep!"—those last three words
suggested by May Massee to emphasize that everyone has been
drawn into the general goodwill at the end of the book.

The early reviews of *Lentil* emphasized the book's drawings.
The *New York Times Book Review* noted that this was one of a
number of recent books in which "the illustrations have played a
part as essential and important as the text, or perhaps an even
more important part, in creating atmosphere and mapping out a
section of this or other countries." The reviewer went on to point
out "The humor and human nature of the drawings," as well as
their "bold line [and] originality."[6]

Certainly McCloskey used bold lines in *Lentil,* as he had in the
George Washington Bicentennial Calendar. And actually he had
considered using woodcuts in *Lentil,* finally deciding that since
the woodcuts would have to be lithographed to reproduce well in
a mass-market book, he might as well start with lithographs, especially since it was an easier medium to work in. The lines, particularly those that outline figures, are very strong and dark,
though drawn with a deftness that suggests characters' flexibility
and motion. This is particularly true of Lentil himself, a sort of
angular, thin, somewhat gangling boy.

All of the production decisions for the book were made in con-
sultation with May Massee and her production unit. With their
advice, McCloskey chose the weight and color of the paper, the
cloth binding, the color of the ink, and the type. In choosing the
type McCloskey had to visualize its character, color, and weight
so that it might be balanced with the lines of the illustrations.
For this, McCloskey worked with Milton Glick, the book designer
at Viking Press, choosing a typeface that seemed to merge with
the lithographic line. McCloskey would later judge that the bal-

ance was so effective that it was difficult to tell where the script ended and the illustration began.[7]

At times the lines of the illustrations suggest that the artist is moving close to caricature. This appears especially in the three pages depicting Colonel Carter and Lentil as they react to Lentil's playing. The dramatically-raised eyebrows, the acute postures, the elongated fingers—all suggest an artistry of exaggeration that matches the exaggerated tall-tale text.[8] This technique also appears in the impossibly puckered faces of the musicians, the wounded antics of the animals who hear Lentil try to sing, and the reactions of Old Sneep. Though McCloskey would use lines as bold as these in his later works, never again would he exaggerate his characters as he does here.

The boldness of line does not, however, mean that McCloskey is not at all subtle in his shading or texture. Particularly in his depictions of Alto, McCloskey uses gradations of gray to suggest shadow, depth, and texture. As the buildings come closer in terms of the viewer's perspective, they become more and more detailed, so that distant objects and buildings are drawn with a few lines that suggest an approximate shape rather than sharply define it. McCloskey would use a similar technique in his depiction of Boston in *Make Way for Ducklings*.

The concluding two-page spread of *Lentil* shows the digging of the foundation for the new hospital. Lentil dominates the right-hand page, standing quite close to the reader and holding his harmonica out in front of him. Up to this point, the narrator of this tale has stood at some distance from the protagonist, using the conventional formulas of story: "In the town of Alto, Ohio, there lived a boy named Lentil. Lentil has a happy life except for one thing—he wanted to sing, but he couldn't!" This opening—with its quick naming, establishment of setting, and definition of the protagonist's main obstacle—is similar to that of many tall tales.

But by the last page the narrator has moved quite close to Lentil, so that the final line of the text—"So you never can tell what will happen when you learn to play the harmonica"—could come from either the narrator of *Lentil*, the character of Lentil, or from McCloskey the author. In a sense, this is a line spoken by all

From *Lentil* by Robert McCloskey. Copyright 1948, renewed © 1968 by Robert McCloskey. All rights reserved. Reprinted by permission of Viking Penguin, a division of Penguin Books USA, Inc., and Robert McCloskey.

three, affirming the eternal possibilities of the simple, the innocent, the unsophisticated.

Homer Price

When *Homer Price* came out in 1943—during the middle of World
War II and the beginning of McCloskey's own time of military
service—the book was hailed by reviewers as a statement of
American principles. The reviewer for the *Saturday Review* suggested that Homer might live in "any town at all as long as it is
in America. No country on earth but the United States could have
produced Homer Price and his fellow citizens."[9] Certainly *Homer
Price* continues McCloskey's evocation of life in a midwestern
small town during the time when he grew up. Whether or not this
evocation was distinctly American was, for McCloskey, perhaps
less important than whether the experience of Homer touched on
the experience of all children who, like Homer and Lentil, come
upon the most marvelous of adventures in the most ordinary of
settings.

Homer Price is actually a collection of six short stories held together by a common setting, a common cast of characters, and
loose references to events in previous stories. McCloskey first
showed May Massee the story that would become "The Case of
the Sensational Scent," believing that that story might represent
a complete work.

> I came in with that first story with a skunk in it and I
> knew it wasn't quite a picture book. I thought it might
> be a storybook. But she thought it should be a story
> among other stories that would be a book. . . . I think she
> was right in that, so she made me go home and write
> three or four more stories to go with it. And it was the
> same with *Centerburg Tales*.[10]

The final collection would comprise six stories about Homer and
the other inhabitants of Centerburg.

The best known of these tales is "The Doughnuts." Here Homer is left in charge of Uncle Ulysses' diner and asked to mix up a batch of doughnuts. In the process Homer is interrupted by the wealthy Miss Enders, who mixes up her own recipe and accidentally drops her diamond bracelet into the batter. When Homer begins making the doughnuts, he finds that the machine will not quit; soon the diner is full of fifteen thousand doughnuts. When Miss Enders returns to retrieve her bracelet, they all face the insuperable problem of finding a bracelet in a room full of doughnuts. The situation is saved when Homer proposes that they offer a reward for finding the bracelet, and soon the townspeople are happily buying and eating doughnuts. Only two hundred doughnuts are left when Rupert Black finds the jewelry.

The other tales deal with Homer's capture of four robbers (he subdues them with the aid of his pet skunk); a revealing encounter with a comic book super hero; a battle between Uncle Telemachus, the Sheriff, and Miss Terwilliger to see who has the longest ball of string; an exotic mousetrap; and the confusion engendered by a suburb of look-alike houses.

McCloskey has suggested that, for him, the process of artistic creation begins with an image and then moves to story: "In drawing your mind can project. For instance, I can look at one doughnut and think of a light snack. I can look at fifteen thousand doughnuts and come up with a story. . . . Most of my friends and neighbors just don't seem to see as I do, even looking at simple little things like a ball of string, a mouse trap, or an abstract expressionist painting."[11] This suggests that in McCloskey's work—even in those texts that are not specifically picture books—the text cannot be separated from the illustration, since the text, in essence, comes out of the illustration.

In keeping with this, each of the stories in *Homer Price* is built around one dominant illustration. These particular illustrations work in the same manner as those of a picture book: they do more than illustrate what is already explicit in a text; they expand, add to, and direct the meaning of the text by suggesting visually what might only have been implicit textually. In "The Case of that Sensational Scent" the dominant illustration is that of Homer in his bedroom, at work on a radio, surrounded by the impedimenta of

From *Homer Price* by Robert McCloskey. Copyright 1943, renewed ©
1971 by Robert McCloskey. All rights reserved. Reprinted by permission
of Viking Penguin, a division of Penguin Books USA, Inc., and Robert
McCloskey.

a boy's life. His posture and activities suggest his resourcefulness and aptness of mind. The skunk asleep in his suitcase foreshadows the crucial turn of events in this story, when Aroma the skunk will crawl into the robbers' suitcase and infect their stolen loot.

The dominant illustration for "The Case of the Cosmic Comic" depicts Homer, his friend Freddy, and little Louis meeting the Super-Duper, a comic book hero. Keen worshippers of this hero, Freddy and Louis are awed, but Homer hangs back. He is more critical; although he is clearly impressed in this scene, he is not as laudatory as the others. His hands are in his pockets and his expression does not suggest worship. The Super-Duper holds an arrogant stance, one arm against his waist, the other stretched out to shake hands. He is completely self-confident. In essence, the whole tale is in this one illustration, for Homer's gentle cynicism will be affirmed, the Super-Duper's arrogance abashed, and Freddy and Louis's worship ended when they see the Super-Duper drive his car into a ditch and get pricked by barbed wire.

Each of the stories has its own dominant illustration that encapsulates the entire tale: the two-page spread of fifteen thousand doughnuts, the enormous ball of string saved by Uncle Telemachus, the exotic mousetrap of Mr. Michael Murphy, the duplicated houses of Enders Heights. They all emphasize the exaggerated, impossible (or at least implausible) elements of McCloskey's stories.

Each of these illustrations is set against a two-page spread that opens each story and depicts the simple chores and activities of small-town life: walking home from school, raking leaves, balancing on the top rail of a fence, drinking an ice-cream soda. The effect of this pairing is an implicit suggestion that the extraordinary events of the tales are occurring in an ordinary setting and are seen from the imaginative viewpoint of a child, a viewpoint that stresses the extraordinary in the ordinary.

James Daugherty's comment in *Horn Book* particularly expressed his enthusiasm for McCloskey's illustrations:

> What I want to speak about especially are the pictures. This guy McCloskey can draw and I don't mean just good

academy. The way these boys fit into their pants, wear their shirts, and the way the folds of their clothes pull with every movement is all there to intensify the vivid humor and real character. This humorous reality pervades even the objects in each scene so that you get the full delicious flavor out of every detail of Homer's room, and the unforgettable barber shop. The double-page drawing of the historical pageant is a classic of a small town celebration. And so one goes over these drawings again and again with renewed delight in all their details.[12]

Daugherty senses the comic delight in the illustrations, delight that comes through details that lend themselves to characterization (Daugherty's specific mention of characterization in his letter to May Massee was deleted for the published version in *Horn Book*).[13]

The illustrations of *Homer Price* pick up many of the same artistic concerns of Lentil. The lines of both books are bold, yet flexible and animated. The sort of "comfortable clutter" McCloskey speaks of which surrounds Homer recalls the detailed hardware store of *Lentil* and looks forward to Mr. Condon's garage in *One Morning in Maine*. The illustrations of both *Lentil* and *Homer Price* evoke small-town life, though *Lentil* does this by focusing on exterior settings while *Homer Price* focuses on interiors, such as the barbershop, Homer's bedroom, and Uncle Ulysses's diner. Both books picture the protagonist as simultaneously a participant in the action and an outside witness to the action principally carried on by the adult world. And both take place in a midwestern setting imaginatively re-created and "remembered" by the author/illustrator.

Homer himself is one in a long line of young male protagonists that McCloskey would draw, a line that would stretch over thirty years from Lentil to Keith Robertson's Henry Reed. All of these protagonists have similar physical characteristics. They are all fairly thin and a bit gangling. They are all at home in small towns and the country. They all seem to have short-cropped, summer haircuts. And they are all clearly children, not adolescents.

The reviewer of the *Saturday Review* suggested that "Homer is a lively, likable boy who is filled with an intense desire to know how everything works. Naturally, he has adventures.[14] Whether or not he wants to know how everything works, he is at least twice shown surrounded by machinery that he enjoys working with. He is able to build radios and fix doughnut makers, and Uncle Ulysses claims that he is clever at working with machinery. What is more important, he is an apt viewer of the adult world, and this is what leads to his adventures.

Linda Silver has suggested that Homer's world, Centerburg, "is archetypical rather than typical, illustrating what was once a common vision of the Midwest: a place of farms and small towns populated by resourceful provincials who worked and played in a spirit of cornball earnestness."[15] For *Homer Price,* how true this version is actually is less important than how true it is mythically. It is within this context of simple innocence that Homer has his being. His world is that of the small town, an archetypal midwestern small town. It seems that everyone is related to everyone else here. The pace is a slow one; the sheriff and Uncle Ulysses and the barber all have time to spend jawing in the barbershop. This is the same world that Lentil moves in, and it is very similar to that of Tree Toad, Trigger, and Henry Reed.

It is a safe, secure world. The one threat comes from Enders Heights, which seems to portend a blight of suburbia. McCloskey uses heavy irony when he has Miss Enders look at the suburb and say "Simply marvelous. . . . Just think. Last week there were only grass and trees and squirrels on this spot."[16] The line stands in stark contrast to the barren, lifeless, hideously mediocre world pictured in the accompanying illustration. But even this is subverted by the humorous peril of a town where all the streets are identical because of their anonymity.

As in Alto, Ohio, nothing very bad happens in Centerburg. As drawn, the villains are more comic than hostile, and when the sheriff does not arrive promptly to arrest them, Homer thwarts them with a pet skunk. The sheriff's spoonerisms define his comic nature, but they also suggest the peaceful character of a town where this figure is the representative of the law. The Super-

Duper drives off a road and into a ditch, but he is not hurt, or perhaps it would be better to say that he is hurt in appropriate ways. Mr. Murphy seems as if he might be threatening, but in the end he too turns out to have been innocuous. Behind all these stories there is the affirmation that though the world is full of potential adventures, it is, in the end, the safe, secure world of childhood presided over by the family. And though his parents are never present (for this is Homer's story, not that of his parents) they stand in the wings behind him.

Because of this, all of the stories end with pleasant resolutions. Almost all of the doughnuts are eaten. The stolen money is returned (though it smells of skunk). The sheriff accedes to the marriage of Uncle Telemachus and Miss Terwilliger, acting as their best man. Even all the trapped mice are released into the countryside. The only story that May Massee questioned was "Mystery Yarn," where she pressed McCloskey to change the ending or write a new story. Marian Rous, who worked under Massee, objected to Miss Terwilliger's cheating, and Massee herself "had a feeling that there should be no reward for cheating," McCloskey recalls.[17] McCloskey resolved the problem by adding a paragraph on how the extra yarn she had used to win had still been saved, though it was not in the ball that had been unwound, so her victory was still achieved by using hoarded string.

Homer's name, like Lentil's, is remembered from McCloskey's own past. Homer was a childhood friend of McCloskey. The name seems to evoke a country hick (of course, Homer is anything but this), but McCloskey's continual play with the classical Homer soon erases any sense of its rusticity. The interplay between the rustic and the classical is established in the very first illustration, where Homer Price stands behind a decapitated bust of the classical Homer. Price is scratched beneath the nameplate, and the fallen head of the blind poet looks with furrowed brow upon the boy who chews on a hayseed and leans nonchalantly against an imaginary fence. (The name Price was May Massee's contribution, named after one of her friends. She suggested the surname for marketing purposes, anticipating that a book simply titled *Homer* would lead to some confusion.)

Oddly enough, 1943 also saw the publication of William Saroyan's *The Human Comedy,* which placed its action in Ithaca, California, and used Homer McCauley as its protagonist. When McCloskey read this novel, he was willing to change all the names in *Homer Price,* but May Massee proposed that he let them stand. This suggests that McCloskey himself did not have any great stake in these names and that their use is more playful than thematic.

McCloskey, once he had chosen this name, remembers that "the other names just followed from it."[18] The most prominent of these is Uncle Ulysses. But Homer also has an Uncle Telemachus, and an Aunt Aggy (whose name recalls Agamemnon) who is married to Ulysses. Both Ulysses and Telemachus swear by Zeus. And "Nothing New Under the Sun (Hardly)" reenacts the story of Ulysses who has his men put wax in their ears to avoid listening to the Sirens. When Homer recounts this tale to Uncle Ulysses, McCloskey plays with the connections between names:

> Just to be on the safe side, Freddy and I asked Doc Pelly to come down to the schoolyard this morning and put cotton in all the children's ears. You know, just like Ulysses, not you, Uncle Ulysses, but the ancient one—the one that Homer wrote about. Not me but the ancient one. (121)

Here Homer Price becomes a character in the event, as well as a teller of the event. Ulysses, a participant in the *Odyssey,* becomes the audience. But though characters' roles are shifted from the *Odyssey* to *Homer Price,* one thing remains consistent: Homer, both the classic and the rustic, tells the story.

In a sense, Homer tells all of these stories, and that is what makes *Homer Price* and *Centerburg Tales* unique among McCloskey's works. In his other books McCloskey works from the vantage point of an adult looking upon the world of a child, and only occasionally does that perspective change. Here, however, the stance is more complicated. Though these tales are told by an older narrator, they are consistently shaped by Homer's own perspective. Nothing happens here that Homer does not observe or participate in. The world the reader sees here is not one about Homer, but one of Homer.

Yet the episodes that occur in *Homer Price* are for the most part not about Homer. Here the reviewer for the *Saturday Review* errs, for Homer does not naturally have adventures; rather, he naturally calls forth adventures. His presence itself seems to be the catalyst for adventures to happen to the world around him. Had these stories been told in the first person, one might have suspected that they emerged from the matrix of Homer's own creative imagination. As they stand, they suggest that Homer's role is to observe the adult world around him, and to observe it with a comic, somewhat naive eye.

For the adult world around Homer is comic, and the adventures that the adults in his world have, while innocuous, suggest a certain humorous inability to control the world around them. In this book adults lose diamond bracelets in doughnut batter, cannot find their houses when signs are not posted, make silly bets based on ludicrous habits. They are, in effect, all Super-Dupers who are constantly getting pricked by barbed wire, or they are all sheriffs, comic types who play out comic roles. Homer observes this comic adult world while the reader observes with him, from his perspective. But to this is added some distancing from Homer, so that the reader does what he would never do: laugh at the adult world.

Though McCloskey's prodding is comic and gentle, there is some meaning behind his jabs that escapes the child Homer. McCloskey pictures the small-town suspicion of a stranger, someone from outside normal experience. He illustrates the dreadful sameness of the suburbs, a sameness that, he was to claim in his 1958 Caldecott Award acceptance, made these suburbs look like hell.[19] He depicts the loneliness in the defeated sheriff. He tells of human arrogance in the person of Miss Elders, an inappropriate clinging to legality as the sheriff tickets the shy Mr. Murphy, the follies of human pride in the townspeople who celebrate the founding of the town but cannot find their own way home. But Homer does not see this darker side of the comic, for he is a child, and sees the adult world and its silliness as a child.

Homer's perspective is mediated through an older narrator. The opening of "The Case of the Sensational Scent"—the first story in the collection—suggests a very present narrator, one who is beginning the story by filling in small details whose significance is not great but that nevertheless establish a context for the tales.

> About two miles outside of Centerburg where route 56 meets route 56A there lives a boy named Homer. Homer's father owns a tourist camp. Homer's mother cooks fried chicken and hamburgers in the lunch room and takes care of the tourist cabins while his father takes care of the filling station. Homer does odd jobs about the place. Sometimes he washes windshields of cars to help his father, and sometimes he sweeps out cabins or takes care of the lunch room to help his mother. (10)

Now certainly none of this is crucial. But in opening the book in this manner McCloskey has established a leisurely narrator who paces the telling of the story slowly, deliberately; there is no headlong rush to get to the main action. The use of the present tense indicates a sense of familiarity, so that the distances between the narrator, the character Homer, and the reader are shortened. It is as if the narrator has known Homer for a time, or as if the reader could travel down route 56A and find Homer's tourist camp. The narration of the story itself does not begin until the fourth paragraph, and its beginning is signaled by a shift in tense: "One night Homer came down and opened the ice box door, and poured a saucer of milk for Tabby and a glass of milk for himself" (10).

For the most part, McCloskey's narrator is restrained and unintrusive, much like Homer himself. Rarely does the narrator break in, and when he does, his observations are similar to those that Homer himself might make. The reader learns that Miss Terwilliger is one of Centerburg's best-loved citizens, "as anyone from Centerburg can tell you" (73). And the reader finds that "after the County Fair, life in Centerburg eases itself back to normal" (94).

The closest union of Homer with the narrator comes in "Mystery Yarn," where the narrator hints at Miss Terwilliger's unraveling her robin's-egg-blue dress to win the contest. The narrator never explicitly announces the unraveling, but leads the reader to this conclusion by noting in succinct fashion how the dress becomes shorter, then changes into a blouse, and finally ends up as blue trim. Only the observant reader will follow this process; many observers in the grandstand do not. But the narrator notes that "there *might* have been a few *very* observing men, who like Homer, knew how she won" (89). The implication here is that Homer, like the narrator, was observant; and this connects both character and narrator to the observant reader.

McCloskey's use of the unintrusive narrator is only one part of his technique in telling these six tales. Another is his frequent references to myths, folktales, and epics. Much of the humor of these tales—particularly that which involves exaggerated characters and situations—can be traced back to counterparts in commonly known folktales. McCloskey transports these tales to Centerburg, Ohio, and retells them by concentrating on Homer's perceptions.

"The Doughnuts," for example, is actually a retelling of the folktale about the sorcerer's apprentice, who seeks to be rid of his task by enchanting a broom to cart water for him. Just as this apprentice finds himself in a virtual deluge, Homer is soon overwhelmed by the doughnuts that quickly fill the diner. McCloskey's repetition of phrases mirrors the endless repetition of doughnuts: "The rings of batter kept right on dropping into the hot fat, and a automatic gadget kept right on turning them over, and another automatic gadget kept right on giving them a little push and the doughnuts kept right on rolling down the little chute, all ready to eat" (58). (This same passage is itself repeated to conclude the story.) While the difficulty is clearly the fault of the apprentice in the folktale, in McCloskey's hands the fault lies with the rather silly and vain adult world; Homer is caught up in the multiplying doughnuts but he is also the one to generate the solution. (Similarly, Homer provides the solution to the multiplying houses in "Wheels of Progress," which reproduce as quickly as the fifteen thousand doughnuts.)

"Mystery Yarn" also suggests connections to earlier tales, and in this case the tale is, appropriately, one from the *Odyssey*. Homer observes as the sheriff and Uncle Telemachus propose a bet that is, at its heart, insulting: whichever has the longest length of string will marry Miss Terwilliger. Penelope faces a similar challenge at the end of the *Odyssey* where the suitors stage a contest with her as the potential prize. Both Penelope and Miss Terwilliger thwart their suitors through the use of their wits, and both enter into a married state, Penelope when Ulysses is revealed, and Miss Terwilliger when she chooses Uncle Telemachus under conditions that she controls.

McCloskey's most evident use of folktale comes in "Nothing New Under the Sun (Hardly)," a title that itself suggests the recurrence of story. Here the characters themselves assert the literary antecedents of their own tale, and they define these antecedents through the medium of their own peculiar interests. The barber judges characters by their hair, and suggests that Mr. Murphy "looks like somebody I've heard about, or read about somewhere. Like somebody out of a book, you understand, Sheriff?" (103). Uncle Ulysses judges by his appetite and notes that "he's a sort of person that I've read about somewhere" (104), echoing the barber. Tony the shoeman argues that "those shoes must have just up and walked right out of the pages of some old dusty book" (104); Mr. Hirsh mentions his storybook clothes; the sheriff researches the problem in the library and concludes that this character is Rip Van Winkle.

All of this turns out to be ironic; Mr. Murphy does have a literary reference but it is not Rip Van Winkle. The reader at first accepts this judgment, despite subtle warnings such as the townspeople's remarking on "how clever the sheriff was at deducing things" (105). The sheriff is not clever, as subsequent events prove. The purported Rip Van Winkle actually turns out to be a Pied Piper. The adult world of the novel does not surmise this; Homer does, and McCloskey makes strong suggestions to the reader about Murphy's character. When the town takes back its payment for his mousetrapping, he drives off followed by the children. The adults panic when they finally realize what role Murphy is playing, but the children have already saved themselves.

Homer has had their ears stuffed with cotton (another reference to the *Odyssey*), and the children follow not because they are compelled to follow, but because of an innocuous curiosity: they want to see the mice released. The potential tragedy suggested by the folktale is thus averted by the observant eye of the protagonist—and the reader.

Through all of this Homer remains the child observer. There are moments when he might have grown into something quite different. He could have given in to disillusionment when he discovers the true nature of the very human Super-Duper; instead, he reacts like a child: he will trade his comic books for a used baseball. He could have given in to a judgmental cynicism when he sees Enders Heights erected; instead, he allows himself to participate in the general jocularity of the town. He is a young boy who does not change, but is, in all of these stories, very much the same, held back from an adolescence that might make him look at the adult world with quite a different eye.

Centerburg Tales

Eight years after *Homer Price*, in 1951, McCloskey returned to Centerburg in his *Centerburg Tales*. (One early sketch for the cover entitles the book *Centerburg Stories*.)[20] The familiar cast of characters appears, taking on their familiar roles as McCloskey uses exaggeration for comic effect. *Centerburg Tales* is divided into seven tales, the first three of which are told by Homer's Grampa Hercules, or Grampa "Herc"; the name, of course, is a continuation of the classical motif established in *Homer Price*. The first tales take place in different periods of American frontier history, ranging from the settling of Ohio to the California Gold Rush. Each chronicles a tall tale from the supposed early life of Grampa Hercules. The fact that Hercules could not have lived in these periods is made irrelevant first by Hercules' indeterminate age (Freddy remarks, "You can't tell whether he's fifty or ninety, to look at him")[21] and then by the nature of Hercules' stories, which make no presumption of absolute historical authenticity.

Notes for the first draft of the introduction of Grampa Hercules suggest McCloskey's conscious desire to associate Hercules with the tall-tale tradition. The notes begin with a reference to Paul Bunyan, the best-known American tall-tale hero.

> Start with a story from Uncle Herc to children in the town square. Paul Punoinn's brother Mike making flapjacks and had some batter left over, poured it on their logs, there wus our logs, all the winter's work, all tangled up in flapjack dough, and whats more, that cussid Mike wus gonna build a fire under em and cook the whole shootin match to a crisp. I just happend to remember as how Paul told me one time that Mike wus ticklish, so I got all the men together and . . .[22]

McCloskey's early draft begins with an objective stance in the first sentence, but the opening of the second moves into a narrative voice. By the close of the second sentence the voice is that of Hercules, who pictures himself as one of Paul Bunyan's loggers. The last sentence breaks off and the idea was not used in the final draft. But the note suggests that Hercules' voice is meant to be that of the teller of tall tales.

These first stories deal with crossing a bump in Curbstone Creek, constructing the exotic "Ride-a-Hide" for which Indians paid hides to be twirled dizzy in a barrel, a town that went by its slowing clock until night became day and day night, and Hopper McThud, who hops back and forth over a creek with bags of gold strung around him. When he takes the gold off to jump in the water to bathe, he accidentally leaps up a three-hundred-foot cliff.

The fourth story is a result of a challenge to the third tale by the men of Centerburg. Hercules is urged to prove his tale by recreating Hopper McThud's feat. He practices by jumping back and forth over a creek while covered with lead tabs and finally does make his fantastic leap, but no one is there to see him. His claim to have jumped nineteen miles to Top Knot, Indiana, is scoffed at until the children of Centerburg rescue his reputation by planting proof in Top Knot.

The other stories are closer to those of *Homer Price* in terms of the participation of Homer. In "Experiment 13" Dulcey Dooner, last seen as a recalcitrant sign poster in *Homer Price,* inherits and plants a vial of seeds. Tended by Homer and Freddy in Dulcey's greenhouse, they quickly grow into giant ragweed plants that threaten to spread the pollen all over town. Homer is the first to recognize the dilemma, but Dulcey forces the town to pay three thousand dollars before he allows the plants to be destroyed. Everything is put to rights, however, when Dulcey is threatened by the imposition of a new seed tax.

The final two tales begin with the arrival of strangers into Centerburg. The first, a flimflam man, sells bottles of "Ever so much more so," which supposedly increases the inherent qualities of virtually anything so that it is soon ever so much more so than it was. When everyone recognizes the swindle, Hercules saves the day through his imagination, and Ulysses empties the entire can by a statue of "Peace," noting "it's really a waste of time to shake it on. We'll just fill it right up to the top and let it keep a runnin' over and soakin' in!" (151).

The final tale deals with a song from a record dropped into Ulysses' juke box by a stranger. Virtually compelled to play it, Homer and Freddy find that they cannot stop singing the tune and even speaking in rhyme. Soon most of the town is chanting the song, and only when Homer finds an antidote in a Mark Twain short story does the singing stop.

Much in *Centerburg Tales* is very similar to *Homer Price.* Most of the characters have appeared before. Homer, Freddy, Ulysses, and the sheriff are constants. Grampa Hercules is introduced into a very prominent role. Homer's parents are again absent, though Mr. Gabby, a minor character from "The Doughnuts," returns to provide an impetus for the tales of Hercules' jump. The librarian makes another cameo appearance, and Dulcy Doner is a bit more prominent. However, the wonderfully poised Miss Terwilliger, now presumably a Mrs. Price by having married Uncle Telemachus, is missing.

Two other characters are introduced from outside the tales, and they appear only in the illustrations: Sal and Jane, McCloskey's own daughters. Sal first appears in the two-page introductory illustration for "Grandpa Hercules," and again beside Hercules while he sits on the monument steps to tell a story (14). (A young boy very similar to Trigger sits in front of her.) She and Jane both appear later in Uncle Ulysses' diner, when Hercules buys all the children doughnuts. Sal peers over Hercules' right shoulder, while Jane, perhaps the younger, reaches in front of Homer for a doughnut, much as she would later reach for an ice-cream cone in *One Morning in Maine* (24). In one sense, these are merely filler characters rounding out a crowd of children. Yet, in another, they suggest a union of McCloskey's childhood in Ohio with his adult life in Maine.

A number of minor characters rush in and out of these stories; sometimes they are merely represented by a name: Buster Buyseps (42), playing on Buster Crabbe, the Olympic swimmer who starred in several Tarzan films; Durpe Donner, playing on the Burpee seed family. Most often such characters instigate the action of the tale, coming from outside to begin some kind of complication. In this sense the salesman in "Ever So Much More So" and the stranger in "Pie and Punch and You-Know-Whats" are inheritors of a tradition begun by Mr. Murphy and Miss Enders in *Homer Price*.

One other common element between the two books is their use of story. While *Homer Price* shows the influence of folktale, *Centerburg Tales* is marked by a reliance upon the tall tale and the stories of Mark Twain. The tales told by Grampa Hercules come out of the western tall-tale tradition with its exaggerated characters and situations, centered on the frontier experience. Hercules and his partners trade with Indians, raft down rivers, and pan for gold in ways that are comic because they are implausible, dramatic, and extreme.

But many of the tales also have their basis in the work of Mark Twain. In certain ways Homer himself is a Tom Sawyerish character, with perhaps less of Tom's mischievousness and giant chivalry. But he is like Tom in his celebration of boyish adventure. The adventures of this collection—both those of Hercules and of Homer himself—reflect the sense of boyish adventure found in

From *Centerburg Tales* by Robert McCloskey. Copyright 1951, renewed © 1979 by Robert McCloskey. All rights reserved. Reprinted by permission of Viking Penguin, a division of Penguin Books USA, Inc., and Robert McCloskey.

specific Twain tales. Hercules' story of jumping while weighted down has a number of details similar to Twain's "The Celebrated Jumping Frog of Calaveras County." Homer himself ascribes his solution in "Pie and Punch and You-Know-Whats" to an unnamed story by Twain.

McCloskey's use of Twain is suggested early on in *Centerburg Tales* by the frontispiece. Here, busts of Homer and Mark Twain stand side by side on a shelf. Homer and Freddy stand next to them, imitating and mocking them by holding a mop and broom to suggest the beard and mustache of Homer and Twain. The blind Homer has his eyes turned away, but Twain stares rather severely at the boys, as though reprimanding them for their irreverence. The opening stands as an announcement that Twain's tales are indeed going to be treated rather irreverently.

The nature of story itself is the subject of much of *Centerburg Tales*; the title indicates a concentration upon story rather than character. Grampa Herc, for example, though he is clearly a char-

acter, is also a virtual incarnation of story: he is consistently identified by the children as a sort of fountainhead of stories, as he
has been for at least two generations. When he is first introduced,
the children gather expectantly, recognizing that almost anything
can remind Hercules of a story.

> "I remember," said Grampa Hercules, "as how one time
> I saved up enough plugs from chewing tobacco to send in
> and get a music box. Played awfully pretty music," he
> said, stroking his chin thoughtfully.
> All the children were watching Grampa Herc closely,
> and they knew when he stroked his chin in just that way,
> he was thinking of a story.
> "Does the music box remind you of a story?" asked
> Ginny Lee impatiently.
> "Can't say as it does," said Grampa Herc.
> "Mebbe chewing tobacco plugs," suggested Freddy
> hopefully.
> "Nope," said Grampa Herc. "But all this bouncin' [of
> balls] and spinnin' [of tops] reminds me of something."
> The old man continued to stroke his wrinkled chin
> thoughtfully while the children seated themselves on the
> steps to listen. (12–13)

From this rather archetypal position of the storyteller surrounded
by expectant children, Grampa Herc begins his first tall tale.

There is an absolute acceptance of these tales by the children
of Centerburg. Perhaps this does not mean that they would all, if
pressed, agree that there was a bump in a physical river, or that
a prospector, when relieved of his burden of gold, could jump three
hundred feet. What it does mean is that the stories are accepted
as part of the world of the imagination, a world that is not subject
to empirical testing or misappropriation. So when Mr. Gabby uses
Grampa Hercules' story as part of an advertising campaign, Hercules claims

> There's not anything wrong with that story in its place.
> These two crazy fellas 're tryin' to put my story in a box

and make it something to eat! The trouble with these advertising people is that they don't know where words and stories stop and what *isn't* words and stories begin. They get it all confused and printed on a fancy package and commence to believe it's every word true. (63–64)

For the children, though, these stories are true in a sense, in that this audience is more than willing—is anxious—to suspend its disbelief. When the story of the three-hundred-foot jump is really put to the test, it is the children who affirm its imaginative reality.

But the adult world is not quite as accepting. The sheriff, speaking of Hercules' stories, claims that "there's some catch to [them], something that's not quite right" (64), and this is the attitude held by much of the adult world, which is sensible and practical. The situation recalls McCloskey's claim. "It gets pretty lonely up here on cloud nine. Or up here on the roof like Old Sneep. And [friends and neighbors] are all down there looking up at me, like I'm some kind of a nut. But I'm not a nut, really, as anybody can see. I have one foot resting on reality, and the other foot firmly planted on a banana peel."[23]

So when Ulysses and the sheriff complain about the reality of Hercules' tale of the sparrows holding back the clock hands, Hercules claims (as might McCloskey), "You two fellas . . . are just like the crazy fella eatin' a doughnut and smackin' his lips over every bite when all of a sudden he commences to worry himself into a case of indigestion over what's become of the hole in the middle!" (38). Max's question about the three-hundred-foot jump—"Is that a *true* story?" (56)—is meaningless in the world of the imagination: of course it is true and, as Hercules notes, "You can't pick that story to pieces" (56).

Hercules rejects a kind of scientific authenticity: "An old storyteller like me can't open his mouth without somebody sayin', 'that ain't accordin' to scientific fact—that ain't been proved,' you say" (71). Homer later asserts this same sentiment: "[Grampa Hercules] thinks that people the age of Uncle Ulysses and the sheriff, and we children too, are living in a scientific age and don't appreciate anything that's not scientifically proved in laboratories with statistics and theories" (77). Such empirical proof, Hercules would claim, is demanding something of a story that is by its nature antithetical to story. When Ulysses and the sheriff complain about Hercules changing the ending of one of the tales, Hercules replies, "That story keeps getting older and changing every year, just like people. The trouble with you fellas is not enough exercise. You're getting older and losing your sense of humor, and this story keeps getting older and better!" (29).

In the end, Hercules' vision of story is triumphant, and he leaves the field of battle with a tale about floating eggs. And at this point the narrator breaks in to affirm Hercules' vision: "The sheriff and Uncle Ulysses didn't say a word, but that's not surprising, because Grampa Hercules had the last words to say in *this* story. He said 'em too, didn't he?" (85). Here the narrator, who is also engaged in the business of telling tales and who will soon be telling tales as tall as those of Grampa Hercules, takes on the same stance as Hercules. He appeals directly to the audience— "didn't he?"—and the use of the contraction "'em" links the narrator through language to Hercules. It is as though the narrator is preparing the reader for the tales to come, which do not use a character as a mediator, suggesting that the reader is to accept the coming tales as Hercules would have his listeners accept his tales.

In the midst of these concerns Homer establishes himself as a figure quite apart from the adult world around him. Here, as in *Homer Price,* Homer is an inquisitive, active boy, who always seems to be around the great and near-great adventures of the small town. In fact, his presence once again seems to impel these events. Often the tales begin with Homer—and the town—in some sort of restful, lethargic state that is interrupted by the arrival of someone from outside immediate experience; the arrival initiates the adventure. Homer plays with tops by the G.A.R. monument in the middle of the town square and suddenly Grampa Hercules appears. He opens the barbershop, complaining "Everything is so usual around here. Seems as though nothing ever happens here any more" (89). (An early draft has the sheriff say "It's time something happened here in Centerburg," but this line was shifted to Homer, since it is unlikely that the sedate sheriff would want anything to start happening.)[24] Soon Dulcey Dooner claims his inheritance and plants the giant ragweed. Homer tends Ulysses' diner and the salesman selling "Ever so much more so" and the stranger with the record come in.

Homer's reaction to the adventures of *Centerburg Tales* is similar to that shown in *Homer Price*. He participates mostly on the fringes of the adventure until it reaches its climax. Like Lentil, he watches as the adult world befuddles itself, and only at the end does he step in to tender a solution. This last is much more pronounced in *Centerburg Tales* than in either *Lentil* or *Homer Price*. While Lentil offered his solution tentatively and hesitantly, a natural impulse offered spontaneously, Homer's solutions are dramatic, made in the midst of conundrums that utterly baffle the adult world around him.

When Dulcey's plants grow, it is Homer who first recognizes that they are ragweed; he is also the one who figures out how the seeds might be safely destroyed: he bakes them into the doughnut batter and feeds it to the postmaster's dog. (The illustration of that dog suggests that it is actually Penny, McCloskey's own dog, that also appears in *One Morning in Maine*.) It is Homer who discovers that the cans of "Ever so much more so" are empty when he and Freddy pry the top off. In addition, he is the one who is first suspicious of the salesman; in the illustration, while the adults watch raptly, Homer eyes the salesman distrustfully (141). Homer later points out that no one had paid for doughnuts while the salesman was there. And finally, it is Homer who comes upon the solution for the incessant singing in the final tale; he is pictured atop a mountain of books, the one figure who can stop the antics of the townspeople.

And so the safe, secure world of Centerburg is protected by the good sense of the child. If the town is endangered from time to time, it is by only innocuous dangers. Imaginative threats, they issue from the creative imagination of childhood, hold exaggerated sway for a time, and then subside into the practical calm of a small town at the junction of routes 56 and 56A.

3

Early Collaboration: Defining a Style

The publication of *Lentil* represented the beginning of two strains
that would repeatedly appear in McCloskey's work. The first is
an intensely personal strain, where McCloskey reaches into his
own memory or looks about at his own family and tells his tales
from those experiences. This strain was to culminate in *Time of
Wonder.* The second is that of the tall tale, where exaggerated
characters encounter extraordinary, dramatic events. This was to
culminate in *Burt Dow: Deep Water Man.*

Yankee Doodle's Cousins

An interest in the tall tale was to lead to McCloskey's first collaborative work: *Yankee Doodle's Cousins* (1941), a collection of
American folklore and tall tales. The war years were to spawn a
number of these collections. Dell McCormick's *Paul Bunyan
Swings His Axe* (1936) and James Cloyd Bowman's *Pecos Bill*
(1937) established the literary form that some of the later collections would take. In 1941 Esther Shepherd published *Paul Bunyan,* a collection of tales about the logger. Walter Blair published
Tall Tale America: A Legendary History of Our Humorous Heroes
in 1944. In that same year Irwin Shapiro published *Yankee Thun-
der, the Legendary Life of Davy Crockett.* And in 1949 Glen

Rounds finished *Ol' Paul, the Mighty Logger.* Aside from the collections of Blair, Shepherd, and McCormick, which were reprinted in the mid–1980s, none of these remain in print. Anne Malcolmson, writing just before World War II, saw her collection as a response to the viewpoint that American folklore was not particularly worthy of study. "The English youngsters are lucky in their national heroes," she laments in the preface. "They have King Arthur and Beowulf and Robin Hood to fight for, each in his own way outrageously congenial to the ten-year-old world."[1] Denying that American folklore is "roughneck," she argued that the heroes of the tall tales belong to the world of children because of "their wildly romantic exaggerations, their quixotic naïveté, their lack of self-consciousness, and their hard-headed adaptability to circumstances" (viii). She concludes that her collection will introduce "Real Americans [who] can help our children identify themselves with the working, democratic, industrial civilization that is America" (ix).

Though this sounds as if the stories are to be manipulated so that they would become the voice of propaganda, this was not to be the case. From the first tale of John Darling on the Erie Canal, Malcolmson is caught up by the intrinsic interest of the tales, and she never foists a heavy didacticism upon them. This stance is supported by McCloskey's many illustrations that center on the humor or poignancy or exaggeration of the tales, not on their evocation of a "working, democratic, industrial civilization." The tales need no purpose other than that which they carry as stories.

Yankee Doodle's Cousins was published in the same year as *Make Way for Ducklings,* but it was an enormously different kind of book. McCloskey came to work at Houghton Mifflin through a contact with a college roommate of his wife, and did the book mostly for the sheer work. When it was finished, he found that the choices of paper and typeface were very limited at Houghton Mifflin at that time, and the book itself was printed on a letterpress. Chagrined, McCloskey noted that "the look and feel was very disappointing."[2]

But reviews for the collection were universally high in praise. Alice Jordan, writing in *Horn Book,* noted the "delightful freshness and freedom" of McCloskey's illustrations.[3] In the *New York*

Times Book Review Ellen Lewis Buell wrote poignantly that "there have been new heroes made for America since this book was published a few weeks ago." She was one of the first critics to note the connection between the exaggeration of the text and that of the illustrations. The stories, she wrote, "have been told with the first requirement of such tales, a hearty enjoyment of their absurdities and extravagances, which Robert McCloskey seems to have shared in making his strong, clear-lined illustrations."[4]

Yankee Doodle's Cousins is one of the most complete collections of American tall tales to come out of this period, but in several ways it is an odd assortment. Macolmson divides the tales by region, dealing with the East, the South, the Mississippi Valley, and the West. Most of these are legitimate tall tales out of American folklore, but others are hybrids. Malcolmson includes a tale set in New Amsterdam but having its literary roots in European folklore, another about the Spanish conquistadors, and another about a legendary healing spring in Pennsylvania. Perhaps the most unifying element of the collection is the uniformity of style in the illustrations.

Despite this eclecticism, most of the stories tell of the tall-tale heroes, many of whom have been forgotten: John Darling barging on the Erie Canal, Joe Magarac squeezing iron beams between his fingers, Stormalong standing five fathoms tall, John Henry driving steel faster than any machine, Tony Beaver commanding his living path, Mike Fink dominating the Mississippi, Febold Feboldson making gargantuan mistakes on Nebraska's Dismal River, Kemp Morgan smelling out oil, Pecos Bill living like a coyote, and Paul Bunyan digging—by accident—the Grand Canyon. All of these narratives are intensely visual because of their exaggerated qualities.

It is to Malcolmson's credit that she restrains her prose and does not let the exaggeration penetrate to her style. While she is not skilled enough to simulate in any way the oral quality of these tales, she is nevertheless able to evoke the quality of wonder inherent in them. Sometimes she does this through evoking the setting: "In the old days Nantucket was a noisy, busy place. Weather-beaten sailors with rings in their ears worked on the docks. They climbed the rigging of whaling ships that came into port from the seven seas. Many of them stomped about the town on wooden legs. Their faces and hands were striped with scars. They were a tough lot" (53). There is a certain romanticism here that evokes the ferocity and hardship and adventure and wonder of life at sea. The final understatement seems almost humorous and in some measure subverts the very information it presents, but the total effect of this passage is a visual one; the reader imagines a town filled with stomping, earringed sailors, and this establishes the setting for a tall tale.

At other times Malcolmson speaks directly to her readers as though she were sharing with them a marvelous tale. "You might expect the mule-boys to be unhappy, living most of their lives underground" (45). Of course, readers do expect this, and though they might not be convinced by her answer—"the mule boys had their fun" (46), she suggests rather naively—they are nevertheless brought into an audience relationship akin to that of the oral storyteller who takes cues from the responses of an audience. Malcolmson introduces the story of Tony Beaver in a similar way.

> You won't find Eel River on any maps. The geographers haven't decided where to put it. . . . It's not hard to visit the camp, however, if you really wish to see it. Just send word to the lumberjack himself by the next jay bird you see, and Tony will send his path after you. (109)

The audience/teller quality is created here by a union of a calm, matter-of-fact voice and folkloric, imaginary material. The reader is asked to participate in the tall tale by becoming a character. Though the narrator soon takes a more traditional stance—"One autumn day long ago . . ." (109)—the reader has already become allied with the wondrous, imaginary elements of this tale.

It is precisely these elements that McCloskey included in his illustrations. The process of bringing the reader into the wonder of these tales starts with the endpapers. There McCloskey pictures Paul Bunyan and his blue ox, Babe, strolling across the countryside, flattening trees as they go. Both have a look of nonchalance about them and both look directly at the reader as if to include the reader in their tale, or to invite the reader along on this journey through American folklore. On her back, Babe carries a number of the characters that will appear in the tales of the collection. These are indistinct, though Pecos Bill and Blackbeard are plainly visible. A knight holding his standard also sits on Babe's back, an intruder in this world of American folklore, but nevertheless a figure that invokes the kind of wonder McCloskey is working toward here. The illustration is printed in a blue ink similar to that of *One Morning in Maine* and *Blueberries for Sal*. It also recalls the colors of the *George Washington Bicentennial Calendar*.

The illustration for the title page is also indicative of the attempt to draw the reader into tales of wonder. McCloskey would often include an illustration on the title page—a spitting clam for *One Morning in Maine,* a resting duck for *Make Way for Ducklings,* a strolling, hayseed-chewing kid for *Homer Price.* Here, McCloskey pictures a young boy crouched on all fours, his ankles crossed. He looks away from us and into the pages of the book. Two hundred pages later the reader discovers that this is Pecos Bill who has just fallen from his wagon and is watching the Conestogas pull away from him around the bend. And while the picture here is poignant, on the title page it has been stripped of its context so that only the picture of a boy is present, and he seems full of expectancy and perhaps even marvel. He anticipates what the reader anticipates.

McCloskey's concern for the reader's perspective is constantly evident throughout the text. The four sections of the book each begin with a double-page illustration introducing the reader to the cultural setting of the region. The illustration for the East shows a harborfront from the late seventeenth or early eighteenth century (xvi). The architectural style of the houses is of old New England—the setting for a number of the tales. And in the background, past a dozen or so barrels waiting to be loaded, a sailor listens to the tales of an old hand. To introduce tales of the South McCloskey pictures an extended black family traveling in a horse-drawn cart beneath a tree draped with Spanish moss (72). The illustration for the Mississippi Valley shows a barge floating lazily down the river while a steamboat chugs against the current in the background (116). One of the characters on the barge yawns dramatically, an expression of the slow life of a bargeman. The illustration for the West has no human characters, but it does include a white mustang who will be the subject of a later tale (182). McCloskey pictures a moonlit pool, an expanse of desert, and the mountains beyond, all under a starry sky. If the other three illustrations had depicted settings ripe for the telling of stories, this pictures a setting ripe for the action of a story.

While these four illustrations attempt to capture something of the cultural settings, the remaining illustrations adhere closely to the stories themselves. They each show the dominant characteristic or action of the principal character, that characteristic or action that makes the protagonist a hero of the tall-tale genre. Joe Magarac stirs molten steel with one arm while forming steel beams through his fingers (28). Davy Crockett calmly rides a bear away from marauding Indians (148). Kemp Morgan sniffs for oil, holding his gun and drill ready (189). Slue-Foot Sue, the bride of Pecos Bill, bounces up and down as the cowboys rush to catch her (220). Paul Bunyan weeps into the grave he had dug for Babe (she was to recover) and leaves behind the Great Salt Lake (256). In each case—and for most of the twenty-eight tales in this collection—the illustration depicts the central character by stressing some exaggerated characteristic.

Part of the exaggeration here comes through the artist's manipulation of line. McCloskey uses this in the illustration of Slue-Foot Sue, as she bounces up and down after being kicked from the back of Widow-Maker, Pecos Bill's horse. Her arms, her legs, the folds of her skirt, the seams of her stockings, her hair—all are drawn with vertical lines to emphasize her alternate ascents and descents. In the illustration for "The Ghost of Dark Hollow Run" the ghost of the schoolmaster leans forward dramatically; his posture is matched by the leaning of the background trees (36). The one vertical element is the birch rod he holds, marking the story's offensive instrument.

A similar use of line comes in the illustration of Stormalong's fight with a giant octopus (65). The entire drawing is angled to stress the pull between Stormalong and the octopus. While Stormalong ties the arms of the octopus into knots, it holds onto two plants to keep its balance; these too match the angle of the pulling. (McCloskey makes one change from the text here, one of his few. The octopus was reputed to have a hundred arms, but this would lead to enormous difficulties in illustration. McCloskey solved the problem by giving it nine arms, thus still making it unnatural but capable of being drawn.)

In their depiction of these exaggerated characteristics, the illustrations become extensions of the narrative rather than mere decoration. They supplement the tales by establishing the visual elements of the stories themselves, so that events are captured in these illustrations, rather than scenes as in the four introductory pictures. And this is in keeping with the tone and meaning of these tales, which stress event over setting, or use setting only as a way of showing event. So McCloskey pictures the aftermath of Blackbeard's shooting of his bos'n, Israel Honds (the illustration makes this a humorous aftermath; the text makes it rather dreadful [95]). Ichabod Paddock is pictured confronting the mermaid and the devil after he is swallowed by the whale; water still drips from him (57). Mike Fink dips the noses of sheep into a bucket of snuff (133). Both exaggerated qualities and exaggerated events are included in these illustrations.

The concentration upon event rather than setting led McCloskey to use a kind of background unique in his illustrations. This might be called an iconographic background, where one or two elements are used to suggest a much larger setting. A wooden floor evokes a poor cottage in New Amsterdam or the deck of Blackbeard's ship (15, 95). One furnace evokes an entire steel factory (28). A small patch of sand, clams, and seaweed evokes the bottom of the ocean (65). A stump and pile of apples evoke an apple orchard (123). In McCloskey's later work—particularly his

Illustration by Robert McCloskey from *Yankee Doodle's Cousins* by Anne Malcolmson. Copyright 1941 by Anne Malcolmson, renewed © 1969 by Anne Malcolmson Storch. Reprinted by permission of Houghton Mifflin Company and Robert McCloskey.

picture books but even in his collaborative work—background
was to be absolutely essential to the meaning and force of a picture. Indeed, the background is crucial to *Make Way for Ducklings,* which came out the same year. But here, where background
is not essential, McCloskey restrains his hand and provides only
what is necessary.

There are two exceptions to the iconographic background,
where the settings are used to indicate a sense of longing and
desolation. The first is of Captain Kidd, who, according to the
tale, became a pirate against his will when his men fired upon
British ships (20). From a bluff he looks over the expanse of ocean
toward his ship. The beach below him is as empty as the ocean,
so that the setting itself suggests his loneliness and isolation. The
second deals with Don Juan de Escobar, one of those who
searched for the Golden Cities of Cibola in the southwestern
United States (205). The landscape here is rocky and vast, dominated by an enormous cactus set in the foreground. In the midst
of this expanse Don Juan is a very tiny, vulnerable figure. Both
of these pictures illustrate romance tales that deal with emotion
rather than tall tales that deal with action. For those tales that
focus, then, on pure plot and exaggeration, McCloskey simplifies
his texture and setting to match the simplicity of the plot lines;
for those tales that examine character more thoroughly, Mc-
Closkey provides a more complex, textured setting.

A number of elements in McCloskey's illustrations make them
aptly suited to the tall-tale genre. One element is the sense of
animation. Many of the characters move in dramatic ways.
McCloskey illustrates John Henry's completing of railroad tracks
just ahead of an oncoming train, seen through his legs (103). Spitting spikes onto the rails, John Henry quickly approaches the
edge of the page, striding directly toward the reader. The result
is an illustration full of quick movement.

Another significant element of these illustrations is their tone.
Often the tales relate marvelous adventures in a very even, unruffled tone, as though there was nothing at all extraordinary
about all this. This same stance appears in a number of the illustrations. When Tony Beaver, for example, finds the orphan path
and takes it home, he has to comb all the cockleburs out of its

grass. In the illustration of this grooming Tony combs the grassy hair of the path's head and parts it above its mushroom ear (108). Blending the ordinary with the extraordinary, McCloskey pictures Tony Beaver completely at ease, intent on the combing, smoking his big black pipe.

Although Tony and his path are alone here, several of the illustrations include animals that don't take a direct part in the action but work as witnesses to it. Often their perspective on the featured character is similar to the reader's perspective. In the illustration for Stormalong's battle with the octopus a school of fish swims by. Their line angles in a different direction from that of the two combatants, and they watch the battle with a bemused look; they observe but do not participate. Indeed, they—like the reader—cannot participate in the action of a tall tale; they belong to a different world.

Though McCloskey would never again illustrate what might be called classic literary tales, his involvement with this collection suggests his interest in the tall tale and in its qualities of exaggeration. He had already seen other children's authors and illustrators who had used this exaggeration to good effect, particularly Robert Lawson in *Mr. Popper's Penguins* (1938) and James Daugherty in *Andy and the Lion* (1938). (Though *Mr. Popper's Penguins* was published with Little, Brown, Inc., both authors, like McCloskey, were to work with May Massee at Viking.) And McCloskey himself had used exaggerated qualities in *Lentil*. He would continue to use these qualities until the two strands of his work begun in *Lentil* (the personal life examined and the tall tale) were separated in the later picture books. *Blueberries for Sal, One Morning in Maine,* and *Time of Wonder* were to carry the personal life and have very little exaggeration. *Burt Dow* was to represent the tall-tale strand and, appropriately, it is the most exaggerated of all of McCloskey's work.

Tree Toad

McCloskey's success with *Lentil* contributed to several offers for illustrating works. One of the first of these was for Bob Davis's

Tree Toad, first published in an unillustrated edition in 1935. This book, actually a collection of stories that first appeared in the *Home Magazine,* attained some popularity upon its publication, but it has now long out of print. The 1942 edition illustrated by McCloskey with a frontispiece by Charles Dana Gibson did little to insure its longevity.

Anne Carroll Moore, writing the foreword to the 1942 edition, recalls that after reading *Tree Toad,* "I claimed it at once as a children's book in the name of all the boys I have ever known, from the brothers with whom I grew up in a Maine village to the many boys of all ages I have known inside and outside the public libraries of the country."[5] Yet *Tree Toad* is not children's literature at all. Certainly it is about the events of childhood, but these events are seen through the mediative eye of an older first-person narrator, who frequently reminds the reader that sixty years separates the telling from the event. The events themselves are placed in a context designed for an adult audience, and consequently *Tree Toad* is better classed with such works as Clarence Day's *Life with Father* (1935) and Frank Gilbreth, Jr., and Ernestine Carey's *Cheaper by the Dozen* (1948) than with children's literature.

As a work of literature, *Tree Toad* suffers from redundancies (caused by the original serial publication of the stories) and by a certain meditative circumlocution that occasionally is humorous, occasionally irritating in its exaggerated blandness. Nevertheless, the adventures of the two boys rival those of Trigger and Henry Reed. Stripped of the narrator's commentary these stories would have the tone of the stories in *Homer Price* or some of the Henry Reed books. Bob, the narrator, is painted green so that he might blend into the landscape and steal pears; for this he is christened Tree Toad. Together with his brother Bill, Bob prays for two white-handled pocketknives and they come flying out of a barn window. Bill stages grand fights with mudballs, a presentation of Doré's Nativity etching, the theft of a blackberry pie, alchemical experiments, and pranks upon the village's adult population. While Davis tells these tales, he holds back the narrator's interventions and allows the tales to stand on their own.

When McCloskey came to illustrate *Tree Toad*, he drew his inspiration from these simple tales, for they are the matter of the book that would actually touch on the experience of the child. Each of the eight episodes begins with a full-page illustration. In addition, McCloskey pictures *Tree Toad* on the spine of the book; he is looking back over his shoulder as though inviting the reader to participate in his adventures. One other illustration accompanies the opening page, this showing Tree Toad and Bill frantically scratching: the effect of a bombardment of prickly pears during a mud fight.

In her preface Anne Carroll Moore makes a curious observation: "That [McCloskey's illustrations] will be in harmony with the delightful revelations of boyhood in California of the 1870's, one has only to recall this artist's pictures for *Lentil*, to know that a true interpreter of American character and scene is behind them" (xvi). If Moore is suggesting that McCloskey can capture the experience of the child in his illustrations, she is undoubtedly correct. If she means, however, that drawing an Ohio small town of the 1940s qualifies McCloskey to draw a landscape three quarters of a century and half a continent away, she is mistaken. None of these illustrations actually evokes the West of the 1870s. In fact, these drawings have few geographical associations and almost no temporal suggestions. The dated clothing alone suggests the period.

Moore goes on, perhaps unconsciously, to subvert the purpose of this edition: "There may be readers of *Tree Toad* who will say that Bob Davis' text is so graphic as to need no pictures. That is true" (xvi). But she concludes that this book about two boys who found in their childhood a time of marvelous adventure affirms the "gift of spontaneous laughter" and the "security of family relationships however nomadic the existence" (xviii), two virtues much to be prized in a time when young boys were leaving childhood behind on the fields of Europe.

McCloskey works at capturing this childhood exuberance in his illustrations. Often he concentrates on Bill as he plans his stratagems and on Tree Toad as he bears the burden of carrying the things off. One illustration pictures a delighted Bill blithely painting a grimacing Tree Toad (2). Another shows Bill, Bob, and two antagonists, all naked, seriously and studiously throwing mud balls at each other (96–97). Two others show Bill directing plays and metallurgical experiments while Bob, the younger brother, watches and admires (62, 200). Each captures a moment in the life of a young boy who is constantly being caught up in the innovative marvels that his older brother devises.

Artistically these illustrations show no new directions for McCloskey. The reader does not sense the involvement of the artist with the text, as in *Trigger John* or *Junket*. The scarcity of illustrations—only ten in almost three hundred pages—limits McCloskey's ability to explore setting and character, and indeed, these illustrations are almost unnecessary, not in Moore's sense, but in the sense that they bring nothing to the text; they decorate rather than illustrate.

Perhaps the sole exception to this is the dramatized Nativity. Bill, sitting on the barn floor, stages the event. Annie Nafsinger is the reluctant Mary; the same figure will appear again as Ginny Lee in *Centerburg Tales*. A sack-enclosed wise man looks on credulously, Tree Toad dangles his legs over a manger, and Mr. Campbell's mule watches in amazement as the event begins. The grouping of the figures, the variety of reactions and expressions, the deft use of several items to suggest a setting, the inclusion of small humorous details (a dangling plate as a halo), all point to more mature illustrations.

The Man Who Lost His Head

One of the most problematic texts that McCloskey was ever to work with was *The Man Who Lost His Head*. Coming as it does after the very visual tales of *Lentil* and *Homer Price*, this text is striking in that much of it is not visual and not particularly suited to the picture book genre. "I used all the tricks I could think of," recalls McCloskey, and the strain is evident in several of the spreads.[6] It is, in fact, a book that is saved from a just anonymity only by virtue of its illustrations.

Claire Hutchet Bishop established herself as a writer of children's literature with *The Five Chinese Brothers* (1938), one of the few books by her that remains in print today. This work was quite popular upon its publication, so when Bishop offered her manuscript of *The Man Who Lost His Head* to May Massee, the editor was anxious to publish the book and perhaps include Bishop in Viking's stable of writers. Massee offered the job of illustration to McCloskey, who agreed to take it on.

The story of *The Man Who Lost His Head* bears some resemblance to that of *The Five Chinese Brothers* in terms of its basic structure: a group of rather naive witnesses observes a series of fantastic episodes, their reactions determining the form of each successive episode. *The Man Who Lost His Head* loses its force where it leaves this pattern and meanders to an unsatisfactory conclusion, unsatisfactory because it is clichéd. It is this meandering purpose that leads to some of the difficulties in the illustrations.

The story opens in the manner of a folktale: "Once upon a time there was a Man who lost his head."[7] The familiar opening clause announces the genre of this work, while the identification of the protagonist only as "Man" suggests the anonymity and loss of identity that the character is about to undergo. Having awakened without his head, the man rummages through his rooms, looking desperately in closets and drawers and garbage pails. In despair, he remembers that yesterday he had gone to the county fair to sell his pig, so he determines to retrace his route.

To get to the fair without being noticed, he first makes a head out of a pumpkin, and then a parsnip; both are too conspicuous. He carves and sands a wooden head and, this in place, he travels to the fair in search of his missing head. Having lost his head, he seems also to have lost his sense of practicality, for instead of seeing only about business while at the fair, he learns to enjoy himself by riding the merry-go-round, watching the tightrope walker, and playing games. (At the games he wins a most inappropriate prize: a shaving mug.) But this loss of practicality carries with it as well a loss of good sense: he almost allows himself to be mauled by a tiger.

He is finally befriended by a tattered boy who believes his story about losing his head; he suggests that he can help since he is "headstrong." The Man describes his own head in minute detail, until the boy recognizes that such a head cannot be found; it must be conjured back. At that point the boy realizes that the Man is dreaming and must be awakened. He wraps rags about his hand, telling the Man that "it is going to be pretty hard on me too," since the boy's very existence depends upon the continuation of the dream. When the boy smacks the man, he wakes up to find himself in his own bed, with "His Own Pinkish Round Ordinary HEAD!"

Bishop's story is in the tall-tale genre and might have been told by Grampa Hercules. It contains the exaggerated characters and situations of the tall tales, as well as the objective and credulous witnesses. The distinction here is that while the narrators of the tall tales generally retain the pretense of truth, the veracity of this story is completely undercut by the conclusion: after all, it has been only a dream. Hercules would never have accepted such an ending, since it calls into question the very foundation of the story.

The first half of the tale seems to work with folkloric motifs, as the Man must make three attempts before he can find an appropriate head. The repetition of key phrases and the predictable reactions of the village people are both familiar folktale patterns. His journey to the fair suggests a quest of sorts, one beset with all sorts of difficulties given his condition. But the conclusion of the tale abandons all of these motifs. The aimless wandering through the fair is only implicitly tied to the loss of the Man's head. The response to the incident with the tiger is out of keeping with the Man's quest, as is his jocular acceptance of the carnival's attractions. The discussion with the tattered boy is almost unbearably long; its repetition becomes tiresome. Here the quick pace of the opening has slowed dramatically, and the momentary action at the conclusion leads only to an unsatisfactory ending, unsatisfactory in that it subverts all that has come before.

The Man Who Lost His Head is marked by careful plays on language. The title itself can be read as a cliché and the village people and the menagerie guard all accuse the Man of losing his head; what they mean figuratively, however, he means literally. The villagers make several unconscious references to heads: "WE have not sold our pig yet. You are ahead," and "Still you sold your pig. That should be much less of a headache." Such references, while comic to the reader, are naturally distressing to the Man.

The most interesting wordplay occurs when the Man acts in ways that he could not possibly act without his head, even assuming the conventions of the tall-tale genre. "He looked under his pillow," the narrator recounts, though of course he has no eyes. He tries to recall where he might have lost his head, though, of course, "it is very hard [to remember] once you have lost your head!" He remembers his journey with his hands and feet. He speaks to various characters, and even goes to see the wild animals. There is no attempt to make the man's plight seem real through the language of the narrator; instead, the language establishes the reality of the substituted heads.

It is the paradox suggested by this wordplay that McCloskey utilizes in his illustrations. Many of the illustrations—particularly those that show no head—picture the protagonist in some position necessitating sight. The cover illustration pictures him striding along a country path, peering through a magnifying glass at tracks that he and the pig had left behind. He looks into a garbage pail in search of his head. He knots a tie while watching himself in a mirror. When he carves a pumpkin head and places it on his shoulder, he looks directly out at the reader, lifting his hat as though to introduce himself. And from this point on, he "sees" through the eyes of his pumpkin, parsnip, and wooden heads. Once this is established, the reader accepts it as one of the conventions of this book, a convention that can only have a reality in a dream fantasy.

At the same time, McCloskey's illustrations suggest that the Man is always aware that he himself is continually being observed. Away from his home, he is under the scrutiny of the village people, who remark upon his unusual heads. Only when he is virtually ignored by them will he proceed to look for his own head: "'How do you do?' asked the village people. And that is all they said to him, so like his own head was the wooden head. So the Man went on to the fair." McCloskey depicts this by giving the Man his first really assured, confident stance as he approaches his inquisitors. On the way to the fair the man is observed by dogs and cows. Once there, he is observed by various vendors, a tiger, and finally by the boy who resolves the problem.

At home, the man is observed by a cat, which is never mentioned in the text. When the man first discovers his missing head, the reader sees the reflection of his rather anxious-looking pet peering at its headless master. Later the cat registers fear during the Man's destructive search through the house, curiosity as the Man reflects upon his loss, shock at the choices of a pumpkin and parsnip for a head, and finally a sort of complacent acceptance of the situation as he turns to play with the Man's pajamas and with a chain dangling from a jackknife. In some ways the cat mirrors the varying reactions of the reader, who also finally comes to accept the head. When the head is restored at the conclusion, however, there is no linkage between cat and reader. The Man holds his curly hair and an ear, as if to authenticate that this is indeed his head; the cat is absent, as though that observer, who had been part of the dream sequence, had been dispelled. The man now observes the reader in the same way that he has himself been observed.

These illustrations suggest McCloskey's growing mastery of line, something which had already begun in *Homer Price.* Whereas in *Lentil* McCloskey had depended upon bold lines that lent themselves to caricature, particularly in his facial expressions, the artist is more subtle here, using thinner lines, space, and shape for his effects. The result is a much greater sense of movement and animation than he had achieved in either *Lentil, Homer Price,* or *Yankee Doodle's Cousins.* This is particularly true of facial expressions. The pumpkin and parsnip and wooden heads all take on many expressions, despite the fact that the expressions are carved on and, consequently, fixed. The heads show embarrassment at being discovered, self-satisfaction at the Man's cleverness, despair at the reaction of the village people, excitement at all the fair booths, fear at the attack of the tiger, hopelessness as the Man realizes that it is unlikely that he will find his head.

Similarly the figures themselves move in a very animated way. Before this McCloskey had often placed characters in striking postures: the puckered mayor in *Lentil,* the drunken Dulcey in *Homer Price.* But in *The Man Who Lost His Head* McCloskey never leaves his characters to stand still. There is an almost breathless quality to this book in that the illustrations consistently show movement up until the final illustration, where the Man is still and in bed. And, of course, this quality is appropriate in a book about a search.

The Man Who Lost His Head represents one of the books in which McCloskey had to be particularly innovative in terms of the relationship between the text and the illustrations. In both *Lentil* and *Make Way for Ducklings* the text had generally been placed at the top of the page, away from the illustration; only a few pages place the text at the bottom. In *The Man Who Lost His Head* McCloskey varies this placement a great deal. Only a few of the illustrations are two-page spreads (all the illustrations in *Lentil* and *Make Way for Ducklings* are two-page spreads). Here the spreads are used to establish setting only. McCloskey uses two spreads to show the villagers: one establishes a country scene, another a small-town scene. Both place the Man far to the left to suggest his separation from the community, a suggestion emphasized by his dark suit that contrasts with the working clothes of the villagers. Another spread establishes the confusion and variety and crowds at the county fair. Each spread places the text either completely above or below the illustration.

In single-page illustrations McCloskey places the text on opposing white pages—a technique that works against the union of text and illustration—or varies the placement of the text in each facing illustration. The effect is to unbalance the reader: there is nothing predictable in the relationship between text and illustration, as there is nothing predictable in this dream world.

All of this comes unraveled in the end, when the text begins to dominate the illustrations. Up until the last two-page spread of the carnival, both text and illustration had worked together to create a secondary world loosely attached to the physical world. But once the tattered boy and the Man begin speaking the text begins to dominate so much that it seems as if this is no longer a picture book. As the pictures gradually get smaller in size, Mc-Closkey draws a series of mustaches and ears to illustrate the unending, repetitive discussion. But these static drawings of a discussion seem to be trying desperately to illustrate something that cannot be illustrated. One drawing from a late dummy moves away from this stasis: while speaking, the boy pulls a long string of tied rags from his pocket; he will use this to awaken the Man.[8] But this was eliminated from the final version, and only at the end of the published text, when the boy strikes the Man to wake him from his dream, do the pictures regain their former size and sense of animation.

The book, then, is only a qualified success; it had long been out of print, though it has recently been re-issued. Perhaps its chief interest lies in the growth it shows in McCloskey as an artist, a growth that would come into play when he turned to picture books like Ruth Sawyer's *Journey Cake, Ho!* and his own *Blueberries for Sal*.

Trigger John's Son

In 1949 Thomas Pendleton Robinson's *Trigger John's Son* was published by Viking; this was a new edition, the first having come in 1934 with no illustrations. McCloskey had read this early edition and later noted that he had wanted to illustrate the book ever since he had read it. The promotional material for this second edition suggested that McCloskey wanted to illustrate *Trigger John's Son* because Trigger reminded him of his own childhood in Ohio. Perhaps this is at least somewhat true. He later recalled that the book appealed to him because it was "very Huck Finnish, very Tom Sawyerish."[9] But more to the point is that Trigger is really one of those in a line of characters who, under McCloskey's pen, would participate in the myth of the midwestern boy.

In this myth the boy is always on the edge of innocence; he

learns about the world—that it is not an easy place to live in—
but it does not affect him, for he is still a child and the world is
still a wonderful place, a marvellous arena where the most extraordinary things might happen. He is an outside boy, and uses
the outside as a place of exploration and an exertion of his independence from the adult world. He is almost always separated
from his parents. He is inventive, both in terms of the mechanical
world and in terms of laying plans for grand—and not-so-grand—
enterprises. And in many ways he is complete in himself. Though
he often identifies himself with a group—a gang or neighboring
kids or a strongly assertive girl who takes up his concerns—he is
content to explore the world by himself, or in company with a dog.
For him, life is a time of wonder, sometimes quiet and sometimes
not so quiet.

Trigger's story, though not written by McCloskey, fully participates in the mythos of the midwestern boy. Shunted from one foster home to another, Trigger determines that he will not be
adopted before he has had a good look at his prospective family.
So when he leaves Calais, Maine, to travel to Beechwood, Pennsylvania, he abandons the passenger train and arrives anony-
mously on another set of boxcars. After an initiatory fight, he
becomes part of the Goosetown gang, a group seen by the citizens
of Beechwood as a bunch of lower-class roughnecks. They bring
him to live with the Old Englishman, who is blind, and there, by
chance at first and then deliberately, he meets George Smith, his
prospective father.

There is an immediate respect and liking between them: once
Trigger comes to live with the Smiths, they band together against
some of the stiffness of Mrs. Smith, who still mourns her own
dead son and tells Trigger that she could never treat him like her
own, one of the most poignantly sad moments of the book. As
Trigger is accepted into the family and then into the town, he
starts a series of adventures all aimed at raising money to get the
Old Englishman to Baltimore, where his eyes might be operated
on. He and the gang gather rattlesnakes as a sideshow, cook
cheese sandwiches as snacks outside a circus, and sell patent
medicine to raise the money.

Some in the town have been anxious to see Trigger fail, however, and when Trigger is accused of instigating a fight, the town turns against him and he is expelled from school. However, this leads Mrs. Smith to assert her own love for Trigger. It forces George Smith to stand up to his boss, Mr. Woodruff, one of those responsible for the expulsion. And it even leads to something of a reversal by Mr. Woodruff, who plans to ask the School Committee to rescind the vote. The effect is all spoiled, however, by a absolutely inappropriate ending, where, in the last two chapters, an aunt never before mentioned suddenly appears and announces that she will take Trigger to Boston, an appropriate place for mallards but not for Trigger. The Smiths are powerless in the face of this *diabolus ex machina,* and Trigger is, in many ways, as alone at the end as he was in the beginning. The ending is inappropriate not because it is a sad ending, but because it is illogical and inconsistent with the characters as they have developed. The fact that Trigger's experience mirrors that of Robinson himself does not redeem the ending.

Despite the ending, reviews of the new edition received praise; most of the reviews focused on the illustrations. *Horn Book* began and ended its list of recommended books for fall of 1949 with the opening and closing illustrations from *Trigger John's Son.*[10] Its review suggested that "Robert McCloskey is the perfect illustrator for this new edition" and commented on the "humor and liveliness of his drawings."[11] In the next issue Anne Carroll Moore wrote that McCloskey gave "life and color in black and white illustrations to a story which called for the liberal pictorial interpretation ... given it." She referred to it as a "thoroughly American storybook," implying that its Americanness comes as much from the pictures as from the text.[12]

McCloskey drew eighty illustrations for the book, using Earl Clifford as the model for Trigger.[13] (He would later use Earl's father, Ferd Clifford, in *One Morning in Maine.*) He spent one entire summer on the illustrations and eventually took them to Italy to finish. As with *Yankee Doodle's Cousins,* the illustration for the title page comes from inside the text. In it Trigger saunters toward the reader, absolutely at ease, whistling, his hands in his pockets.[14] Later the reader finds that this illustrates his return from an exploratory trip beyond the Old Englishman's cabin, but here the mountainous background places him in the context of the natural world. This might be paired with the final illustration of Trigger; this time he runs away from the reader, a leave-taking of both the Smiths and the reader. The cover illustration similarly engages the reader. Trigger sits just inside the Smiths' shed, whittling. Behind him is the midwestern architecture of Beechwood. Trigger looks directly at the reader, smiling, inviting into his world of simple innocence.

The pictures invoke a kind of world, a world of simple values, hardship and joy, naiveté and courage. McCloskey has set his drawings about the turn of the century and he uses many of the almost mythic elements of a small town to illustrate Beechwood. The illustration of the main street has an ice-cream parlor (mandatory in the myth of the archetypal main street), a general store, and a drugstore. Horse-drawn carts stand in front of all these. Behind them is a house whose filigreed roof establishes the period. Tallest of all is the church, whose steeple rises above the other buildings (68–69). This same small-town setting is evoked during the sale of the patent medicine. Dogs run past a woman carrying a wicker basket, a group of overalled men consider buying, and a trombone and drum sound to announce the sale (206–7).

The illustrations emphasize the slow summer life of the town. The Goosetown gang gathers around the slippery elm to decide how to raise money for the Old Englishman. Grouped around the tree, they lie on the ground, look up at the sky, and chew on hay; one is propped on elbows; Trigger lies on his stomach (174). As in many of the illustrations, the pose of the characters suggests the meaning of the scene. It is an unhurried life they lead. And it is a boy's world; the reader's perspective in both the text and the illustrations never leaves that of Trigger.

As in much of McCloskey's work, the illustrations function in a narrative sense, adding elements at times that do not appear in the text but are appropriate to an illustration. When Trigger and the gang fry cheese sandwiches outside the circus, they are immediately approached by a clown and animal trainer; the door to the circus owner's wagon has just opened. An elephant objects to the smell in the background and another character rushes toward them with two buckets of water (150–51). All of this happens simultaneously and leads to a great sense of confusion; hardly any of it is in the text.

Opposed to this is an equally narrative picture. The Old Englishman leads the Goosetown gang through the forest and into the hills; they carry the old Englishman's fox, which they will set free since the old man is leaving for his eye operation. They walk into the light from the darkness of the woods (216–17). This is the most blatantly symbolic picture McCloskey would ever include in his children's illustrations, for the morning light suggests the new freedom of the fox, of the Old Englishman, and even of Trigger, who is about to find a home. There is order and stillness and solemnity about this picture.

Perhaps the most important element of these pictures is in the way they depict relationships. In many of McCloskey's earlier drawings characters were isolated or shown in one-dimensional relationships. But his illustrations here evoke more complex relationships. Many of these focus on the growing relationship between Trigger and George Smith. At first they are mistrustful of each other, though Smith longs for a son. When first pictured together, they face in opposite directions; Smith looks at Trigger with a sideways glance. Despite this opposition, they are united in that they are both whittling, and both are whittling the same kind of shavings the Old Englishman uses for his fires (90). Later, when they have established an alliance, they are shown together dunking their heads into a half hogshead of water (109, 194). Their common activity and state suggest their growing relationship. At the conclusion of the tale, when the entire town, it seems, has turned against Trigger, he and George Smith are seen walking along together, in the exact same posture, not speaking, but reassuring each other by their very presence (264, 278). These last scenes are not in the text, though the development of the characters leads the reader to believe that it must have been so.

In illustrating this book McCloskey was in some ways continuing the adventures of Homer Price; he would continue them further in the Henry Reed tales. There is a certain family resem-

Illustration by Robert McCloskey from *Trigger John's Son* by Tom Robinson. Copyright 1949 by Tom Robinson and Robert McCloskey, renewed © 1977 by the Estate of Tom Robinson and Robert McCloskey. All rights reserved. Reprinted by permission of Viking Penguin, a division of Penguin Books USA, Inc., and Robert McCloskey.

blance between all these midwestern characters, but more important is a certain spiritual resemblance. And spiritual is not meant to suggest religious qualities here, but instead those qualities of innocence, wonder, fair play, and justice that are important to all of these characters.

Trigger John's Son, like *Lentil, Homer Price,* and even *Junket,* is a story about childhood, a time before the coming of age and all its attendant anxieties. This does not mean that Trigger does not have real troubles—he, not unlike Mr. and Mrs. Mallard, is searching for a home—but everything he encounters is seen from the perspective of a child working within the framework of what is, for the most part, a safe and secure world. And in many ways the world of these characters has itself not come of age; it has remained frozen in that mythic time of gentle gangs and good-hearted shivarees and ice-cream-parlored main streets that probably only exists as a cultural myth but is nonetheless real for all that.

4

Make Way for Ducklings: The Bound World of the Public Garden

Published by Viking Press in 1941, *Make Way for Ducklings* was to mark McCloskey's entrance into some of the most important themes of his children's books. It was to become his most-lauded picture book, the book that would firmly establish him as a children's book author and illustrator. Nevertheless, in the opening to his acceptance speech for the Caldecott Award that *Make Way for Ducklings* won, McCloskey claimed that "I'm just an artist who, among other things, does children's literature."[1]

While attending art school in Boston, McCloskey had already begun to conceive the idea of *Make Way for Ducklings*.

> I used to live just around the corner from Louisburg Square. I used to walk through the square almost every day, then walk down Beacon Hill and through the Public Garden on my way to art school. And I used to see these ducks and feed them. There were the children, the bicycles, the bridges, and the policemen, swan boats. Looking back on it now, they all seemed to be waiting around, ready to be put in a picture book. But it was not until four years later that I wrote the first draft to *Make Way for Ducklings*.[2]

When McCloskey brought the draft in to May Massee, he had never studied duck anatomy. He suggested that he did not know how to draw ducklings and had a great deal of work to do. "She admitted as how that was so," McCloskey recalls.[3]

While working on *Make Way for Ducklings,* McCloskey shared a studio on West Twelfth Street in Greenwich Village with Marc Simont. From here he made trips to Boston to sketch the background drawings. He spent two years drawing ducks and ducklings, at first working only with stuffed mallards. He eventually bought two sets of live ducklings, one in the Washington Square Market in New York, the other in Boston. He and Simont drew lots to see which bedroom would house the ducklings. Simont lost, and each sunrise they would waken him with their quacking. "Today if I were doing this book, I would find a spot in the country next to the mallards, and we would live happily together. But then I had to be in the center, where the action was, and so I brought the ducks to New York," McCloskey said later.[4]

Even after the sketches were finished McCloskey had difficulties with the ducklings. Marc Simont recalls his attempts to get rid of the beasties.

> Bob McCloskey could never have passed as a native New Yorker. The author-to-be of the *Centerburg Tales* had Middle West written all over him, complete with large frame, crew cut, and honest face. All these attributes are well received in most places, but not necessarily when you're trying to sell some ducks to a New York butcher.
>
> "They'll probably gyp me," I remember him saying when he left the studio with the ducks, "but I don't care. I'll take anything they give me."
>
> When he came back to the studio hours later, still with the ducks, he looked terrible.
>
> "I couldn't sell them," he said, "so I tried to give them away, and that was worse."
>
> Robert McCloskey, exhausted and sweaty, holding on to that dripping crate of ducks, was a pitiful sight. But

even in defeat he was denied the dignity of peace and quiet. The ducks were raising the roof. It had been a long day for them too, and they were starving.[5]

Eventually the ducks were settled with a friend in Cornwall, Connecticut.

The story is as old as the Edenic expulsion: the search for a home. Mr. and Mrs. Mallard fly over eastern Massachusetts evaluating possible nesting sites, but Mrs. Mallard rejects each one for fear of foxes and turtles. They settle for a time on an island in Boston's Public Garden; at first they are attracted by the peanuts thrown by visitors on the swan boats. But when a bicycle almost runs Mr. Mallard down, they look elsewhere, finally settling for a small island in the Charles River. Soon they have nested and hatched a family of eight ducklings.

When Mr. Mallard goes off to explore the river, promising to meet them in the Public Garden, Mrs. Mallard teaches her ducklings to follow her in line. After a time, they swim to the shore, cross the Back Bay, and reach the Garden, always protected by the policeman Michael and his friends. And "when they reached the pond and swam across to the little island, there was Mr. Mallard waiting for them, just as he had promised."[6]

In his Caldecott speech McCloskey explained that *Make Way for Ducklings* represented a growth in his perception of art itself. In the Public Garden he had first seen the mallards and watched the passengers feed them from the swan boats. "I liked these ducks and I enjoyed feeding them peanuts, all good relaxation, I thought, for a mind heavy-laden with great art thoughts." McCloskey, never imagining the ducks were anything but a diversion from the serious business of life, returned to New York to work on *Lentil*. "It was about this time," he writes, "that I started to draw and paint everything and anything. I lost my ability for making up droopy trees and the anatomy of non-existent dragons and gazelles. Why, I even drew ducks." He had left behind what he called "a lot of ham ideas" about art.[7]

Four years after he left he returned to Boston and the idea for *Make Way for Ducklings* began to take shape. He had noticed the traffic problems that the ducks caused and heard stories about them, one involving a family of ducks that had stopped traffic with great aplomb as they crossed the street. He left Boston with a dummy that he was to show to May Massee. Over the next year he wrote and revised the story of such a family of mallards, crafting it so that it became not merely an amusing anecdote, but a tale that showcased the major themes that would dominate all of his picture books.

The dummy began with the Mallards returning to Boston, rather than arriving for the first time.

> When Mr. and Mrs. Mallard saw the sign saying "23 miles to Boston Air Port" they flew just a bit faster. They had been living in the south all winter, and were anxious to get home to Boston, because it is a lovely place in the spring. When they reached the city they flew over the dome of the state house and looked down on the familiar red brick houses of Louisburg Square and then flew back to their home, which was on an island in the center of the public garden pond. Yes, it was pleasant to be in Boston in the spring, and to swim in the pond, and to follow the swan boats, quacking loudly at the man who sits inside of the swan to make it run, and to eat the peanuts that the passengers would drop into the water.[8]

All of these items—Louisburg Square, the State House, the swan boats—would be included in the final text, but they would be placed later in the book, along with the corresponding pictures of Boston. In the dummy Boston is familiar to the Mallards, and they are simply coming home and revisiting old haunts. But in the final text McCloskey was to emphasize the search for a home. He was also to eliminate the line stressing how Boston was pleasant in the spring, a line that would also close the dummy. Though Boston is indeed pleasant in the final pages of *Make Way for Ducklings*, it has been made pleasant only by the secure home that the Mallards have found.

In the dummy McCloskey has the Mallards lay their eggs on

the Charles River island because of the debris on the bottom of the pond in the Public Garden. After the ducklings are hatched, Mrs. Mallard teaches them what not to eat and they prepare to return to the Public Garden.

> She led the way into the water, and, followed by Mary, Martha, Phillys, Theodore, Beatrice, Alice, George, and John, they all swam to the bank of the river and walked across the park on the riverbank until they came to the driveway. But there were so many cars that it was impossible for them to cross safely to the other side. All the drivers were in a hurry to get to their work or to buy things in the stores, and they honked their horns at Mrs. Mallard every time she would step from the sidewalk, so Mrs. Mallard sat on the curb and "honked" back and all of the ducklings quacked just as loud as their little quackers could quack.

Much of this text is eliminated in the final version, replaced by the illustration that shows the same action suggested by words in the dummy. But McCloskey seems unsure about the role of Mr. Mallard. When they leave the Charles River island, Mr. Mallard is flying protectively above them, though an "x" has been drawn through him. When Mrs. Mallard confronts the cars, Mr. Mallard hovers overhead again. He disappears and does not appear again with his family until they have entered the Public Garden and have turned to take leave of the policemen: "They all turned around just inside the gate and said thank you to the policemen, while Father Mallard quacked his gratitude from above." Mr. Mallard himself seems to be unsure of his position with regard to the family. This nebulous role is replaced by a much clearer one in the final text, where Mr. Mallard becomes a symbol of the family unity and security that Mrs. Mallard is trying to establish.

The final line of the dummy's text recalls its beginning: "Ah me! Boston is indeed a lovely place in the spring." The first two references to this fact had come from the consciousness of the Mallards. This last, though, seems to be coming from a reflective narrator who has told the story and now reflects upon its meaning. It represented an enormous departure from the previous stance and was cut in the final text.

McCloskey spent two years of study for the illustrations. He researched mallard anatomy at the Museum of Natural History in New York. At the Museum's library he "found a top view of a duck's cranium, with minute measurements and a rough estimate of how many years ago ducks were fish. But hidden somewhere I found valuable information of the molting and mating habits of mallards."[9] He also studied mallards with Dr. George M. Sutton, an ornithologist at Cornell, examining especially the wings, bills, and feet.

McCloskey filled sketch pads with pictures of stuffed mallards and their habitats. But these were not living birds; he could not derive the animated qualities of ducklings from stuffed models. So he went back to Boston, back to the Public Garden. And there he took up again what had once been a diversion; he fed peanuts to the ducks, watching and sketching as they swam back and forth, lifted and fluttered tail feathers as they searched the bottom, flew off the pond and, wings held back and webbed feet outstretched, landed again.

The ducks which McCloskey eventually purchased to use as models were not precisely mallards. "I tried to get ducks that looked as much mallard as possible. But those in the market were largely puddleduck. My drawings show the same kind of mix-up, I guess. Children don't care, but ornithologists turn a feather when they see them."[10] In any case he bundled the ducklings into a carton and, with this quacking package, took the subway back to the Greenwich Village studio he was sharing with Marc Simont. Simont, McCloskey recalls, "was distinctly not interested."[11]

During the preliminary stage in the book, the two artists would have sixteen ducks living with them, twelve of them ducklings. "I spent the next weeks on my hands and knees, armed with a box of Kleenex and a sketch book, following ducks around the studio and observing them in the bath tub."[12] They sloshed water from the tub, leading to complaints from the apartment downstairs.

(McCloskey would later comment on "what splashing and house-maid's knee is behind each nonchalant stroke of that duck's wing!"[13]) They wandered off as he sketched one preening itself. They huddled together instead of in a line—as McCloskey wanted them. And they moved too fast. The solution for their rapid movement was an unorthodox one. "The only thing that worked was red wine. They loved it and went into slow motion right away."[14] McCloskey later recalled that the male mallard became quite addicted to the wine and would chase away the female so that he might have all of it.[15]

McCloskey went back to Boston to get the background sketches for the Public Garden, the State House and Beacon Hill, Louisburg Square, and the Charles River. When he returned he brought back six more ducks and continued to fill sketchbooks "with happy ducklings, sad ducklings, inquisitive ducklings, bored ducklings, running, walking, standing, sitting, stretching, swimming, scratching, sleeping ducklings."[16] Most of these poses would appear in the final book. And the changes he saw as the ducklings quickly grew would also be incorporated.

Fifty years later Marc Simont would vividly recall McCloskey's work with these ducklings:

> Bob made dozens of drawings of the ducks in every position except flying, and there was the problem. How was he going to draw an extended wing or a view from beneath? He tried wrapping one of the ducks in a towel secured with a safety pin, then he placed it on the couch with the head sticking out over the edge. Before he could grab pencil and paper, stretch out on his back on the floor, and look up at it, it had wriggled free.[17]

McCloskey was to draw hundreds of sketches for the book; these are now housed in the Boston Public Library.

One result of the months of duck cohabitation was a change in the names of the characters. Instead of ordinary names, McCloskey gave them names more fitting to their own elocution: Jack, Kack, Lack, Mack, Nack, Ouack, Pack, and—perhaps most appropriate—Quack. He later noted that these characters believed that the Caldecott Medal rightfully belonged to them, since the book was about them. In the end, the ducklings, along with the Mallards and the artist, agreed to leave the medal on the book's cover.[18]

At first, McCloskey had wanted to do *Make Way for Ducklings* in color, but May Massee convinced him otherwise. In the early days of their association Massee was not convinced that he had the expertise to use color. She told him, "Now, you have a lot of coloring in your black and white, but . . . your colors are not bright enough, there's something heavy about them."[19] In addition, McCloskey had not done any three-color separations, and the technology for photographing such separations was only crude. Beyond these reasons, however, was the enormous expense of producing a book in color. (One colored drawing still exists; it matches the aerial view of the Public Garden as the ducklings trail behind the swan boat.)[20] Eventually the book was published in monochrome on a very weighty, off-white paper made especially for *Make Way for Ducklings* and chosen by McCloskey and May Massee.

For the final drawings McCloskey used a grease pencil to draw on grained zinc plates. Since no changes could be made in these plates, the drawings had to be exact; they also had to be precisely the same size as those that would eventually appear in the final book. This was especially difficult since the dark pencil did not show up well against the dark plates. Proofs in black ink were made from these plates, and then larger press plates were made from these proofs. The plates were treated so that ink would adhere to parts that were supposed to print and water would adhere to the blank spaces. When the zinc plates wore down, Viking used photolithography to cast new plates from a set of the original proofs made from the zinc plates that McCloskey had prepared. Both drawings and text were printed in a dark sepia. (This is not true of the German version, *Familie Schnack,* in which the text is printed in the same green as the background for the cover.)

Though McCloskey was pleased with the final book, he was not pleased about the cover. He drew a preliminary sketch of the mallards grouped together, but during production Morris Coleman assigned the task of copying that drawing onto acetate to another artist in his office. "I wince every time I see it because none of those strokes are the way I would have done it; none of the ducks are mine."[21] In addition, McCloskey was displeased with the dark green cover.

But the reviews were almost universally favorable and enthusiastic. "The Boston Public Garden has never appeared in more attractive guise than in this engaging book," wrote Alice Jordan in *Horn Book*.[22] "Robert McCloskey's unusual and stunning pictures will long be a delight for their fun as well as their spirit of place." Ellen Lewis Buell, in the *New York Times Book Review*, called the book "one of the merriest we have had in a long time," noting particularly the "fine large pictures, strongly drawn, which, for all their economy of line, have a wealth of detail so that one turns the pages again and again to be sure not to miss a single bit of the fun."[23] Warren Chappell—the only dissenting voice—suggested that "the cleverness of [McCloskey's] crayon has some tendency to cheapen the whole very capable effect," but also allowed that the "drawings have a great deal of variety of interest, achieved through a change of scale and pace."[24] And the *New Yorker* recommended the book by stressing its emphasis on the search for security, this review coming on 6 December, 1941, the last day that any American would feel secure for quite some time.[25]

But Anne Carroll Moore, writing in the same issue of *Horn Book,* was most perceptive in her understanding of things to come. "McCloskey," she wrote, "takes the city of Boston for his background and in a series of large lithograph drawings reveals his sure instinct for the beauty of wild life and that of the city and a sure knowledge of ducks and their ways. . . . There are some very beautiful drawings in this book which are prophetic of future work in the picture book field."[26] She was, as it turned out, quite right, particularly in her assessment of his instinct for wildlife; McCloskey would never again turn to a city for a background.

Viking Press published *Make Way for Ducklings* in the same year that Houghton Mifflin published *Yankee Doodle's Cousins,* but they represent two completely different approaches to the role of art in children's literature. McCloskey's illustrations in *Yankee Doodle's Cousins* are supplementary to the text; they don't contribute to the meaning of the book as much as they take their cues from the text and reproduce a humorous scene already worked in the prose. (This would not be the case in all of McCloskey's collaborative work.) But *Make Way for Ducklings* is first a picture book, and so the illustrations are absolutely integral to the book's meaning; indeed, they carry as much meaning as any of the text.

Perhaps their closest point of contact is in the exaggerated movement of the characters. And even this is relatively minor in *Make Way for Ducklings*. While extraordinary postures appear in most of the illustrations for *Yankee Doodle's Cousins*, they appear only infrequently in *Make Way for Ducklings*. The ferocious intensity of the boy on the bike and the corresponding expressions of surprise and anger on the Mallards' faces, the sprinting Michael rushing to stop traffic, the expressions of wonder and surprise and humor on those who see the duckling procession toward the Public Garden—these represent the few uses of exaggeration in the illustrations. For the most part, the illustrations for *Make Way for Ducklings* are much more realistic, particularly in their depiction of the landscape of Boston and of the Mallards themselves.

But there are other significant differences in these illustrations, generally deriving from the different qualities of the two books. While those for *Yankee Doodle's Cousins* isolate the principal character of the tale and force the reader's attention to that character, those for *Make Way for Ducklings* show characters in relation to each other, to their setting, and to their antagonists. Mr. and Mrs. Mallard flying and nesting together, the ducklings following their mother, all the Mallards watched over by Michael—none of the Mallards are ever seen in isolation; the concentration is always on the family unit.

The illustrations are themselves much more developed, particularly with regard to the backgrounds. Instead of the iconographic settings of *Yankee Doodle's Cousins*, the settings in *Make Way for Ducklings* are much fuller. Boston and the Public Garden are drawn in a gentle guise, with deft strokes. The Mallards are never seen without reference to this setting; in many ways the setting is the story, for it presents the opposition that must be overcome if the family is to be reunited at the end of the book. The setting allows McCloskey to experiment with texture (particularly in the outlines of the buildings and the Public Garden, and the feathers of the mallards) and with light and shadow—elements that are unimportant in *Yankee Doodle's Cousins*. But perhaps most significant of all is McCloskey's handling of point of view. The illustrations of the tall-tale characters are almost always seen from a straight-on perspective. But in *Make Way for Ducklings* McCloskey manipulates the point of view so that we often see the setting from the Mallards' perspective. The result of this is that images are essential to meaning; the illustrations themselves carry the story.

Make Way for Ducklings also has some strong connections to *Lentil*. Although they are unlike in terms of subject matter, *Lentil* and *Make Way for Ducklings* are quite similar in their structure. Like *Lentil*, *Make Way for Ducklings* is divided into two connected halves, each containing a rising action, climax, and resolution. The first half deals with the Mallards' search for a nesting place free from marauding turtles, foxes, and bicycles. The second deals with the journey of Mrs. Mallard and the eight young ducklings. Both stories begin with the ducks in some form of danger from both the natural and human world and end with the security represented by the family unit and an island.

The final resolution—the secure and simple life on the island in the Boston Public Garden—works to complete both halves by solving the initial problem: where shall the Mallards raise their ducklings? This question is resolved in both halves, so that the repetition of the story emphasizes the theme of security; structure supplements meaning. This represents a growth in the use of this form, for in *Lentil,* though the music of the harmonica is a common resolution for both halves of the tale, the first half is for the most part expository in nature when the book is viewed as a whole: it sets up the solution to Sneep's nastiness in the second half of the book. But in *Make Way for Ducklings* the repetitive structure intermingles the two stories so that they become, in their final effect on the reader, one story.

That story has, at its heart, the search for and the finding of assurance and security—and in *Make Way for Ducklings* these are found in the context of the family. This concern for security opens the book, as the Mallards reject what appears to be a peaceful countryside scene because of the potential foxes and turtles. They similarly reject the Public Garden (at first) because of the bicycles. When the Mallards find the island in the middle of the Charles River, both they and the reader recognize that they have found a place of safety. It is a safety that will later be paralleled by their life on the island in the Public Garden.

When Mr. Mallard leaves to explore the rest of the river, some of that security vanishes with the breaking of the family unit. After a suitable time of training, when Mrs. Mallard taught the ducklings "to walk in a line, to come when they were called, and to keep a safe distance from bikes and scooters and other things with wheels," they swim to the shore of the Charles and journey through the Back Bay district, once again to find a place of security. The dangers they pass on the way to the Public Garden are overcome by their own proud assertiveness—and the watchful care of Michael and his cohorts. Actually the traffic is more a source of frustration than danger, and when Mrs. Mallard crosses the street in front of the traffic that Michael is holding back, she has a haughtiness that would fit the grandest Beacon Hill dowager. This episode hints at a concern that McCloskey would later deal with in *Homer Price* and *Centerburg Tales*: the effects, both humorous and threatening, of uncontrolled mechanization.

When they arrive and swim to the island, the search for security ends, for "there was Mr. Mallard, waiting for them, just as he had promised." The family unit is complete; the promise has been kept. The island is established as a home. And in the last two sentences of the book McCloskey switches to the present tense to suggest the omnipresent security of the family: "All day long they follow the swan boats and eat peanuts. And when night falls, they swim to their little island and go to sleep."

Michael's role is crucial here; he is the friend and protector. But

McCloskey's other human characters are an ambivalent lot. There is no clear division here between the worlds of the children and the adults. Both are peopled with figures who are interested in, annoyed by, and unaware of the ducks. The children on the swan boat are the ones who throw the peanuts; the adults look indifferently ahead. But it is a child who almost runs down Mr. Mallard in the Public Garden. Later, the cars are peopled by adults who, for the most part, look straight ahead with a fierce indifference. But these are stopped by policemen, who allow the family to continue its journey. The witnesses of that journey—both children and adults—are all surprised and even moved by this evidence of the natural world in the midst of the city. It is a moment of societal leveling, where the proper old lady and the man who swept the streets and the child are united in their wonder.

What these characters witness is the subversion of the rigors and rules of the city—essentially what the Public Garden tries to do for Boston, or what any commons tries to do for any city. The Mallards reject the countryside scene that opens the book and that seems perfectly appropriate from the viewpoint of the reader. They accept what seems to be an inappropriate setting and force the reader to see it through their eyes, so that Boston, for all its traffic and highrises, becomes a soft and secure place, a place of abundance, free from all the natural enemies of the Mallards. McCloskey later suggested that "Boston has a soft feel. It's not just a chiseled out city."[27] The distinctions between city and country, adult world and child's world, are merged in this family of ducklings.

McCloskey has commented that "you have to rather think like a duck when you put together a book like [Make Way for Ducklings]."[28] The result was what he called in his Caldecott acceptance speech a "duck's-eye view" of things, where everything in the book is perceived from the angle of vision of the Mallards.[29] The opening landscape, the islands in the Public Garden and the Charles River, the State House on Beacon Hill, Louisburg Square—all are seen from high in the air, from the perspective of the Mallards as they search for a safe home. The point of view in the illustrations supports the meaning of the story, which is told in a controlled prose by a narrator whose perspective never leaves that of the Mallard family. This continues until the final two pages, where the narrator draws back from them and leaves them to their island isolation and the soft darkness.

Frequently the reader is at ground level with the Mallards, so that the world is something the reader—and the ducklings and any child—must peer up at. Speaking of this perspective, McCloskey has suggested that to achieve it realistically "you think of being just as small as you can, and just thinking back to your own childhood can help you with that." This perspective is seen particularly in the illustration of the bridge that spans the Charles River, a gargantuan sentinel over the resting Mallards. But this perspective suggests that the world is sometimes a rather dangerous place—bicycles and cars loom larger in this world and call for a protector like Michael, who is never anything but enormous in the book, as he would be from the Mallards' point of view.

At times McCloskey is playful with the point of view. One of the final pictures shows the Mallards following the swan boats and eating peanuts, seen from high in the air. Here the reader is forced to a duck's-eye view, though no duck is seeing what the reader sees. At other times, McCloskey brings us to ground level to see the new ducklings close up, but the two times we get so close, one or two ducklings hide behind either a clump of grasses or Mrs. Mallard and look directly at the reader, suggesting that there is something intrusive about the duck's-eye view and that the ducklings would prefer some distancing.

If this perspective points out the dangers of their world, it also emphasizes the security of it. Both islands are seen from above to stress their isolation; the human world never intrudes into either of these havens. Both islands are overlooked by bridges, which seem to keep the human world at a distance. And both—particularly that in the Public Garden—are drawn with soft strokes that suggest a homey, secure comfort.

McCloskey manipulates the spacing of the ducklings to suggest

From *Make Way for Ducklings* by Robert McCloskey. Copyright 1941, renewed © 1969 by Robert McCloskey. All rights reserved. Reprinted by permission of Viking Penguin, a division of Penguin Books USA, Inc.

One day the ducklings hatched out. First came Jack, then Kack, and then Lack, then Mack and Nack and Ouack and Pack and Quack. Mr. and Mrs. Mallard were bursting with pride. It was a great responsibility taking care of so many ducklings, and it kept them very busy.

this same need for security. In most of the illustrations they look in six or eight different ways, yet they are all either in a swarm around Mrs. Mallard or in line behind her. Only twice are all the ducklings focused in the same direction; both times they are focused on images of security. In the first, Mr. Mallard leaves his family to explore the river. They all watch him, some rather tentatively, as he swims away. Later, their positions will be reversed as the ducklings and Mrs. Mallard swim to Mr. Mallard, who watches intently from his island. The second instance comes inside the entrance to the Public Garden, when the family turns to thank the four policemen who protected them on Beacon Hill.

This security is also emphasized in the transformation of Boston from city into country. The buildings of Beacon Hill are often drawn in impressionistically, with only a few strokes of their roofs and upper stories suggesting their entirety. The industrial sector along the Charles River is kept far away, its unpleasantness nullified by distance. The building we come closest to is the Corner Book Shop, textured so that its bricks are soft and its front absolutely nonthreatening. And once inside the Public Garden, any potentially harsh city images are muted by the abundant trees and the pleasant evening shadows.

In a letter to Pauline Bloom, May Massee wrote that *"Make Way for Ducklings* appeals because it's first of all a good story, very close to nature, introducing traffic problems which all children meet these days. And then it has so much humor in the pictures that the whole story is lifted up by the drawings."[30] McCloskey pictures the ducklings in the multifarious ways that he had sketched them, so that they preen themselves, thrust out their chests, stretch their necks, plunge under the water, lean over each other, chase insects, flap wings, rush after each other with floppy webbed feet. They quack shrilly at the traffic, strut proudly in front of the stopped cars, and peer back at those who watch them. They are always moving, always animated. And despite Quack's persistent lateness, they are always all in the picture (though in one illustration Kack is hidden behind a tire). Their playfulness and order, vivacity and obedience, posturing and humor suggest the aptness of the title.

And perhaps this humor is at the heart of *Make Way for Duck-lings,* for McCloskey the artist is most anxious that his material be enjoyed. "Yes, I'm working on children's illustrations. I'm proud of that. But I'm still for hire—to paint, sculpt, whittle, or blast if it's on some job that will bring pleasure and be used, whether it be in a bank, post office, or chicken coop."[31]

5

The Maine Books: The Bound World of the New England Coast

When *Blueberries for Sal* was published, the first of the four picture books that McCloskey would set in Maine, Anne Carroll Moore began her column in the *Horn Book* by recognizing the significance of McCloskey's career in children's literature.

> Robert McCloskey has kept on drawing in terms of his own observation and perception. He has known the American child at different stages of growth, beginning with the zestful Lentil and his harmonica, the forerunner of Homer Price. It may seem strange to those who think of McCloskey chiefly in terms of *Lentil* and *Homer Price* that he should be able to render so sensitive a perception of the three-year-old Sally and her interests as will never cause her embarrassment in years to come. . . .
>
> It requires no special gift of imagination to realize how easily Robert McCloskey could have been signed up for a comic strip. That we still have artists who scorn a market place where this and that can be made to order rather than created is a tribute to those editors of chil-

dren's books who have stood by creative artists rather than manufactured art.[1]

In later years McCloskey himself would take up this theme, arguing that children's literature was not something to be dashed off as quickly and cheaply as possible. Instead, like any art, it needed to be given time so that it might be true to its subject, close to the experience of the child and produced with care and quality.

In terms of his own art, the publication of *Blueberries for Sal* in 1948 announced a number of departures for McCloskey. It represented a movement away from the Midwest and the life of the small town to the coast of Maine and a life that is ruled by the tide. It represents—at least until *Burt Dow*—a movement away from the tall-tale genre. And it represents a move away from a concentration on McCloskey's own past to a concentration on himself and his wife and the adventures of their daughters. As he notes of *Blueberries for Sal*, "here's my acquiring of a family."[2]

Certainly the tone of the Maine books is not one of exaggerated humor; this is especially true of the first three picture books that deal specifically with the McCloskey family. The tone of *Blueberries for Sal, One Morning in Maine*, and *Time of Wonder* is quiet, gentle, and restrained. There is no poking fun at the protagonist as McCloskey chronicles typical events in the life of a child growing up in Maine: gathering blueberries, rowing across the bay, digging for clams, playing on the beach, riding out a storm. There is a certain degree of seriousness here, as though this were the important stuff of life and not to be undercut with overt humor.

But despite the change in locale and tone, these picture books do not represent a change in structure or in theme. They are still episodic, *Blueberries for Sal* the simplest, *Time of Wonder* the most complex. Thematically these books assert the same kind of assurance and security in the family first represented in *Make Way for Ducklings*. They also suggest the bounded worlds in *Lentil, Homer Price*, and *Make Way for Ducklings*: two of the Maine books are set on islands whose physical boundaries suggest familial closeness and protection. The final aspect of the island setting on the reader is not unlike the final effect of the safe island in the Boston Public Garden.

Blueberries for Sal

Blueberries for Sal comes out of McCloskey's summer experiences in Maine, interweaving a tale of his wife and daughter Sal, picking berries on Blueberry Hill, with the similar story of Little Bear and his mother who come to the hill to eat blueberries and store up food for the winter. Neither Little Sal nor Little Bear is as accomplished a berry picker as their mother, and soon they lag behind and begin to wander. Eventually they begin to follow the wrong parent, so that "Little Bear and Little Sal's mother and Little Sal and Little Bear's mother were all mixed up with each other among the blueberries on Blueberry Hill."[3] Little Bear's mother discovers the switch when she hears Little Sal drop three blueberries in her pail; the other error is discovered when Little Bear takes a Tremendous Mouthful of blueberries. The mothers soon find their appropriate children, and while the bears head off full of food for next winter, Little Sal and her mother go back to the waiting car with a pail of blueberries to can for next winter.

The focus of *Blueberries for Sal*—as it would be in the next two Maine books—is on the small events of childhood; it is this that strikes the reader even before the larger story of the mix-up of Little Sal and Little Bear. As Sal begins to pick blueberries, she confronts the rather wearisome fact that it is difficult to pick enough blueberries to cover the bottom of one's pail; it is much more pleasant to eat them. The result is that she can never get beyond having three or four berries in her pail.

To this common element of childhood are added numerous other small but intensely familiar events. Little Sal shows a childlike joy in discovery as she wanders over Blueberry Hill and discovers a group of crows (she watches them in delight and wonder) and Mother Bear. Sal also shows a delight in sound itself, as she listens to the "kuplink, kuplank, kuplunk" of the berries falling into her pail. And later she delights in helping her mother can the berries for the winter.

The tightness of this story explains a revision in the original dummy. McCloskey had planned to close with a section where Mother explains to Sal how they can berries for the winter and Mother Bear explains to Little Bear how they eat berries for the winter. Six months pass and McCloskey pictures Sal sledding down a hill, eating a dessert of preserved blueberries, and going to sleep. The final illustration showed the bears asleep in their den; the narrator notes that they will not feel hunger, nor will they wake up until next spring.[4] But all of this is moving away from the immediate experience, as well as from the consciousness of the child. It is also extraneous to the themes of the book. All this material was cut, and the book ended with an image of a homey kitchen.

The visual details contribute to the reader's sense that this book is about the familiar territory of childhood. One of the straps on Sal's overalls refuses to stay on her shoulder. Her unruly hair sprouts in several directions. Her fingers are not nimble enough to pick only one berry out of her mother's pail, just as Little Bear will later be unable to take only a small mouthful. And throughout the book she is not willing to muster the perseverance necessary to fill an entire pail of blueberries.

Little Bear shares this familiar territory of childhood, for though he and his mother are clearly bears, they also exhibit many of the same traits as Little Sal and her mother. Little Bear also gets a bit bored and wanders away. He too delights in discovery and in sound. In fact, all four characters are highly symmetrical in their relationships and in their goals. They are, in effect, on Blueberry Hill for the same purpose, and they find the same experiences. Still, the focus remains principally on Sal, as suggested by McCloskey's rejection of an early title: *Blueberries for Sal (And for Bears Too)*.

The final effect of the story of this book is one of reassurance and security that stems from the relationship between the mother and child. Like the world of the island in *Make Way for Ducklings,* this is a secure world; there is no real danger here. Part of this

From *Blueberries for Sal* by Robert McCloskey. Copyright 1948, renewed
© 1976 by Robert McCloskey. All rights reserved. Reprinted by permission of Viking Penguin, a division of Penguin Books USA, Inc., and Robert McCloskey.

security comes from the innocence of childlike responses. Little
Sal looks at Little Bear's mother and Little Bear looks at Little
Sal's mother in complete innocence, spawned by an unawareness
of any kind of enmity. It is the adults who are shy of the children
and who, McCloskey writes, are "old enough to be shy" of little
bears or little girls. Appropriately the adult mothers never meet
in this book, since they have lost the ability to give the innocent
kinds of responses that Little Bear and Little Sal can give.[5]
    When McCloskey came to draw the closest encounter between
Little Sal and Mother Bear, he wished to include as much of
Mother Bear in the illustration as possible (43). May Massee argued that he had drawn the bear too close to Sal, suggesting that
such proximity would frighten a child. McCloskey then moved

Mother Bear back one quarter of an inch.[6] In addition, he eliminated material from the text would suggest too close a meeting
between bear and child. Part of the original draft showed a conscious desire on Sal's part to befriend the bear.

> Little Bear's mother heard Sal walking along behind and
> thought it was Little Bear. And she said "Garfroofh—Fa
> Garfooth—Fa—Gruff! (To Little Bears this means "Keep
> on eating berries, and berries, and still more berries!")
> "I will pick some berries for this bear and make
> friends" thought Little Sal, and she picked three berries
> and dropped them kuplink, kuplank, kaplunk in her
> small tin pail."[7]

In the final text Sal follows Mother Bear without consciously deciding to befriend her; Mother Bear is yet another element of the
natural world that fascinates Sal. For the reader, and perhaps
even for Sal, Mother Bear is also a representative of maternal
security.

The largest part of the security of this world comes in the re-
lations between mother and child. Both mothers show surprise
and shock when they discover the mix-up of their children; both
show relief and delight when they hear the "kuplink, kuplank,
kuplunk" or the rustling in the bushes that reveals their child.
And in the end Little Bear and Little Sal are back with their appropriate mothers and everything is back in its proper place.

> Little Bear and his mother went home down one side of
> Blueberry Hill, eating blueberries all the way, and full of
> food stored up for next winter.
> And Little Sal and her mother went down the other
> side of Blueberry Hill, picking berries all the way, and
> drove home with food to can for next winter—a whole
> pail of blueberries and three more besides. (54–55)

The symmetrical resolution to the day's expedition suggests an
appropriate, happy, and safe ending for both sets of characters.
The fittingness of this final resolution is mirrored in the end

pages of the book. Here Sal and her mother can the berries, and the kitchen is filled with bags of sugar, mason jars, and a complex plated old stove modeled after one owned by Ruth Sawyer in Hancock, Maine. Sal strings the rubber jar lids along her arm as her mother pours the berries into the jars. The busy kitchen, with two cats on the plank floor, a geranium on the windowsill, polka-dotted curtains, and steaming kettles all suggest a homey, secure world.[8]

The voice of the narrator who mediates this world is the most distinct voice that McCloskey had as yet used in any of his picture books. In telling the story of McCloskey's own family the narrator speaks with a gentle familiarity and an assured air. Despite one reviewer's claim that the story "has just enough hint of danger to be exciting but maintain good feelings,"[9] the narrator's voice never suggests fearfulness as it might have when Sal encounters Mother Bear. The voice never suggests an overriding suspense, as it might have as the mixed-up situation develops. Instead, the rhythmic repetitions of the narrator create a tone of calm humor. "Little Bear and Little Sal's mother and Little Sal and Little Bear's mother were all mixed up with each other among the blueberries on Blueberry Hill" (38). The repetition of the two names and of "blueberries" reflects the confused situation on the hill, but points out its humor rather than any apparent danger.

Throughout *Blueberries for Sal* the repetition reflects the similarity of experience for Sal and Little Bear. Both characters have precisely the same stories, told in the same language and with the same tone. Both mothers, who single-mindedly pursue blueberries, are "old enough to be shy of bears" (48) or people, "even very small bears like Little Bear" (48) or "even a very small person like Little Sal" (42). Both mothers know "just what made that kind of a noise" when they go to find their children. In no other book will McCloskey equate the experience of the plot with the experience of the language in quite this same way. The effect is to establish a symmetry between the two, as there is a symmetry within the plot structure.

The narrator of *Blueberries for Sal,* then, is quite subtly drawn. Clearly the narrator is not a child who, like Homer Price, observes and comments upon the adult world. Nor is the narrator a child with a limited ability to organize and give meaning to an experience. Instead, this is an outside, adult narrator (it is tempting to say it is meant to be McCloskey himself) who sees both the worlds of the adult and the child, participates in both those worlds, and notes the differences, particularly in terms of characters' reactions to situations.

In terms of the artistry of this work, McCloskey uses more detailed lines than in either *Lentil* or *Make Way for Ducklings*. The accumulated lines define the laden blueberry bushes, which McCloskey drew from his own experience and from detailed studies of blueberry bushes in what was then called *National Geographic Magazine*.[10] Eventually the lines merge into shaded and darker areas that suggest spruce woods. These lines give texture and depth to the single color: dark blue, appropriate to a book about blueberry picking, though the same color would later be used for *One Morning in Maine*.

McCloskey carefully manipulates the size of the characters in terms of the page. Sal and Little Bear, though they may dominate a page when they are alone, are very small when they are together with the adults. In the first page, for example, Sal and her mother walk toward the reader, looking directly from the page. McCloskey here introduces his family as though they were coming onto a stage, a technique also used in the opening of *Journey Cake, Ho!* This manipulation of size suggests the child's vision where so many things in the adult are so big and unwieldy.

This is the first McCloskey picture book where the natural landscape plays a very dominant role. (The landscape of *Make Way for Ducklings* is certainly significant, but its effect is a somewhat ironic one in that the city setting is used by the mallards as a natural habitat.) Since all of the action takes place on Blueberry Hill, the hill itself becomes a character. McCloskey pictures its trees, its contours, its jutting rocks, its stumps, and, of course, its blueberries. It is a place where the natural world and the human world come into close contact, and though the two bears are anthropomorphized, the rest of the natural world is as it might be found in a Maine landscape. (In *One Morning in Maine* McCloskey would abandon anthropomorphism entirely.)

The bears, the crows, the partridges all suggest quite a different world from the small town of Alto or the city of Boston. They depict a life closer to the natural world, and McCloskey would continue in this vein for the remainder of his picture books, all of which were to be set in Maine. *Blueberries for Sal* was to garner a Caldecott Honor, behind Berta and Elmer Hader's *The Big Snow,* another book about the natural world. But more important than that, it established the setting for the rest of McCloskey's picture books.

One Morning in Maine

Four years after *Blueberries for Sal* Viking published McCloskey's *One Morning in Maine.* This too was to garner a Caldecott Honor, this time behind Lynd Ward's *The Biggest Bear.* The second book in what might be called McCloskey's trilogy on the life of his family in Maine, it continues and expands many of the concerns and artistic techniques of *Blueberries for Sal.*

Like *Blueberries for Sal, One Morning in Maine* focuses on the individual family in a bound environment—this time, an island rather than a hillside. The narrative focus is again principally on Sal, though here she is older and somewhat in charge of her younger sister, Jane. The color is similar to that of *Blueberries for Sal*: a blueberry blue. But in *One Morning in Maine* there is a much greater sense of texture, depth, and shading. McCloskey would later add much more texture—and color—in the third Maine book, *Time of Wonder.*

One Morning in Maine begins with a concentration on Sal. It evokes a fairy-tale setting with its overtones of "Once upon a time." At the same time, it proclaims the importance of the story's realistic setting.

> One morning in Maine, Sal woke up. She peeked over the top of the covers. The bright sunlight made her blink so she pulled the covers up and was just about to go back to sleep when she remembered "today is the day I am going to Buck's Harbor with my father!"

Sal pushed back the covers, hopped out of bed, put on
her robe and slippers, and hurried out into the hall.[11]

From the very beginning the story centers on the trip to Buck's
Harbor from Sal's point of view.

While brushing teeth with Jane, Sal discovers that one of her
teeth is loose and believes that it will spoil her plans. Comforted
when her mother sees it as a sign of growing up, Sal makes a
secret wish on the tooth and heads out to find her father, who is
digging clams. She announces her loose tooth to a fish hawk, a
loon, a seal, sea gulls, and finally her father. But the tooth is lost
while Sal is digging clams, and with it goes her secret wish.

Hope is revived, however, when she finds a fallen gull feather
and makes her wish on that. She and her father leave the clams
with Sal's mother and, together with Jane, head across the bay
and into Buck's Harbor; her father must row across when the motor will not start. In town, Mr. Condon replaces the motor's spark
plug and Sal uses the old one to make a wish for Jane. When they
go to buy supplies, Mr. Condon's brother (who runs the store)
greets them and gives each of the girls an ice-cream cone to com-
pensate for the loose tooth—the fulfillment of the secret wishes.
Then they all head home, Sal clutching a gull's feather and Jane
the spark plug, to have clam chowder for lunch.

In terms of sheer plot, very little happens in *One Morning in
Maine*. The reader looks through the eyes of a young girl and sees,
together with Sal, the interest, complexity, and beauty of the
coast of Maine. Though Sal is not the narrator, her consciousness
is clearly the mediator between the action and the reader, for
nothing happens in this book that does not happen to and through
her. She is the one who makes her connections between the dis-
parate elements of a loose tooth, a gull's feather, and a spark
plug—connections that structure the entire story. She is the one
the reader accompanies across the island, across the bay, and into
Buck's Harbor. Her single-minded concentration on Buck's Harbor and the potential there for the fulfillment of her secret wish
is the strongest driving element behind the plot.

Revisions in drafts for *One Morning in Maine* suggest that this concentration on the voyage to Buck's Harbor became more important and dominant as McCloskey and May Massee worked on the book. A late draft has a significantly different opening that delays the reference to the coming trip across the bay.

> One morning, Sal woke up and stretched.
>
> From the very minute she woke up, even before she opened her eyes, she had a feeling that something was *different*! She looked around the room, wondering what was changed. The lamp and the dresser looked just like always, so did her stuffed donkey who had only one ear because the other had come loose and got lost. Her books were all on the shelf and through the window the sun was shining on the trees and water. She hopped out of bed and looked in her closet, but no, nothing was different in there. All of her clothes and shoes were in their usual places and her suitcase and hat were still right up there on the top shelf.[12]

Though this passage evokes a world—Sal's bedroom—it is a world not particularly relevant to the coast of Maine with which the book deals. The prominence of the trip is missing, though there is the emphasis on Sal's consciousness.

In comparing *One Morning in Maine* to *Blueberries for Sal* it is the development of this consciousness that is perhaps most significant. Sal has grown physically, and a reader might expect to see growth in other areas as well. This is precisely what McCloskey shows. In *Blueberries for Sal* Sal's world was close about her: there was the hill and the kitchen, all governed by the protective presence of her mother. In *One Morning in Maine,* however, this has changed as the circle of her experience increases in size. She is now comfortable with two worlds: the island and Buck's Harbor. The first principally involves her immediate family; the second involves a set of adult friends who react to her with a certain amount of adult condescension but also with real affection.

Sal's world has expanded, as have her experiences and responsibilities. She now digs clams with her father, though, as in *Blue-*

berries for Sal, she does not contribute particularly much to the family larder. She takes care of her infant sister, eagerly taking on the role of an older child as she admonishes her sister who would like another ice-cream cone: "Besides, Jane, two ice-cream cones would ruin your appetite" (63). And since this is a book about a child discovering the marvelous world about her, all on a single morning in Maine, it is appropriate that the focus of the book stays on Sal, or perhaps it would be better to say that Sal focuses the book. Her questions, her discoveries, her observations all come to the reader through a mediating narrator who tells the story of her perceptions during one morning in Maine.

As with *Make Way for Ducklings* and *Blueberries for Sal,* an underlying assumption of *One Morning in Maine* is that the characters are in a secure world and that that security issues from the family. Though *Make Way for Ducklings* is about the search for that security, here it is established—as it would also be in *Time of Wonder.* At each crisis of the book—and these, from a child's perspective, are real crises—a parent is there to offer sound solutions. When Sal finds her tooth is loose and believes that she will not be able to go to Buck's Harbor, her mother uses it as a sign that Sal is growing up.

> "Why, Sal," said her mother, "that's nothing to worry about. That means that today you've become a big girl. Everybody's baby teeth get loose and come out when they grow up. A nice new bigger and better tooth will grow in when this one comes out." (12)

Similarly her father reassures her when the tooth falls out and is lost.

> "That's too bad," her father sympathized. "But you are growing into a big girl, and big girls don't cry about a thing like that. They wait for another tooth to come loose and make a wish on that one." (37)

The emphasis on growing older here suggests the relationship between the first two Maine books, but it also suggests a strong familial bond. In the illustrations for these incidents both parents are kneeling or are crouched so that they are on the same level as Sal, a sign of how seriously they take her concerns.

Buck's Harbor is also a secure world. A small collection of a general store, a gas station, a church, and a few houses, it is a familiar place for Sal and Jane. The cluttered garage of Mr. Condon—reminiscent of Homer's bedroom—is a place to explore and to climb. It is also the place to resolve the one adult difficulty, the broken motor. Russ Condon's store is a place to be good-naturedly kidded and to be treated to an ice-cream cone. For Sal and Jane, it is the place where wishes are fulfilled.

The final page shows a return to the island home. As in *Make Way for Ducklings,* the island here represents a bound world, which accounts for some of its feeling of security. The distance to Buck's Harbor is an important element in these characters' lives, an element that calls for a certain degree of self-dependence. At the same time, it is a world that calls for a recognition of the interrelatedness of the family within the natural surroundings, a relationship strongly suggested by each page.

The illustrations are dominated by images of the natural landscape. This is particularly true of the island home, which, in addition to the family, is frequented by mocking loons, curious seals, and ravenous gulls and fish hawks. Sal is often pictured on a rocky shore bordered by ancient pines; she is simply one other inhabitant in this natural landscape. And she is as at home here as any other inhabitant, as her skipping posture suggests (25). There is, in short, an absolute union of the lives of this family and the natural world, and it is that union that causes so much joy and wonder on this one morning.

Although the color of the illustrations of *One Morning in Maine* is very similar to that of *Blueberries for Sal,* the texturing of strokes in the later book yields many more shades than in the earlier work. Here the color suggests not blueberries, but the sea itself and a life lived in close quarters with the sea. The monochrome blue emphasizes the ever-present closeness of the water and its unceasing influence on this family. *One Morning in Maine* represents McCloskey's last use of this single-color approach, and

and started on down the shore to help her father dig clams.

From *One Morning in Maine* by Robert McCloskey. Copyright 1952, re-newed © 1980 by Robert McCloskey. All rights reserved. Reprinted by permission of Viking Penguin, a division of Penguin Books USA, Inc., and Robert McCloskey.

it is his most effective use, surpassing even that of *Make Way for Ducklings*. The images of the island are evocative mostly because of the texture of the rocks softened by the tides, the sparse grass, the sturdy trees, and the ever-changing sea.

One Morning in Maine is the first book in which McCloskey himself appears as an adult character. McCloskey is, first, the author and illustrator of the text, and as such he is creating a tale of his own family, re-creating a single morning. His illustrations do not exactly reproduce his island, or his house, or Buck's Harbor, or Swain's Cove. But all of these elements are recast to create an artistic and imaginative unity on each page.

In addition, he has also created a narrator who is close to the sensibilities of Sal and who also re-creates, giving meaning and order to a series of what might first be construed as random events. It is this narrator's voice who notes that Sal "started on down the shore to help her father dig clams" (25), establishing a very distinct distance between the narrator and McCloskey himself. It is also this narrator who informs the reader of some elements of the McCloskey household: the reader learns that the dog's name is Penny. But this same narrator also withholds information: the family cat, Mozzarella, appears but is never named in the text.

At the same time, McCloskey is also a character. While he is digging clams with Sal, the reader hears him respond. In Buck's Harbor, when he is no longer central to Sal's consciousness, he is more in the background, so that the reader is removed from him. Since this is Sal's story, his role is principally a supportive one, but he is still characterized. His facial expressions suggest a certain purposefulness in activity, as well as a deep interest in the children.

Generally these roles remain separate, but at times they combine and, in combining, break down some of the barriers between a text and a reader. When Sal loses her tooth, for example, she looks directly at her father to show the gap (36). In each of the three illustrations prior to this, the character McCloskey has been positioned to Sal's left. Now the reader's perspective is manipulated so that Sal's father is outside the boundary of the picture. The result is that when Sal looks at her father, she now also looks directly at the reader. The illustrator has manipulated the character so that the reader has taken on the role of that character and interprets the story in the same manner as Sal's father.

In the final illustration of the book McCloskey himself looks out at the reader, breaking the normal conventions of a character's abilities. This view cannot be accounted for by suggesting that he is looking back to Buck's Harbor, since the blank sky and water which runs to the edge of the pages has obscured that view. Instead, McCloskey combines the role of a character in a book piloting a boat, McCloskey the author interacting with his reader, and McCloskey the narrator bringing closure to a plot. This union would find similar, even more complex expressions in *Time of Wonder.*

From *One Morning in Maine* by Robert McCloskey. Copyright 1952, re-newed © 1980 by Robert McCloskey. All rights reserved. Reprinted by permission of Viking Penguin, a division of Penguin Books USA, Inc., and Robert McCloskey.

Time of Wonder

If one were to read through the Caldecott Medal acceptance speeches over the past fifty years, one is hardly likely to find an angrier speech than that delivered by McCloskey upon his acceptance of his second Caldecott Medal. The first artist to win the award twice,[13] McCloskey used his acceptance to call for a general recognition of what might be called the unnaturally ugly in America, which, he argued, stemmed from a lack of artists and designers.

"I should like to clamor for the teaching of drawing and design to every child, right along with reading and writing," McCloskey begins. "I think it is most important for everyone really to see and evaluate pictures and really to see and evaluate his surroundings."[14] He goes on to decry the deceit of pictures used in propagandistic advertising, but then comes to the major concern of the speech—the closest link to *Time of Wonder*, which is mentioned only once at the beginning of the speech. "Until a few years ago, almost all design had its roots and inspiration in nature. But now there is another inspiration—the machine with its forms, its repetition, its rhythm."[15]

This is not the same kind of machine that appears in Homer Price's bedroom or Mr. Condon's garage or in Grandpa Herc's Hide-a-Ride. McCloskey is instead attacking the unregulated products of a machine-dominated mindset—technology without any design but repetition. McCloskey had already gently satirized housing developments that reflected this mindset in *Homer Price*, where he drew houses "as alike as a hundred doughnuts."[16] But in this Caldecott acceptance speech he is not so gentle: "And how do the houses look, lined up row after row, aerial to aerial in the housing development of an unimaginative builder? They look like hell!" He concludes that "our land with government of the people, by the people, for the people is fast acquiring an environment of machines, by machines, for machines."[17]

The expression of this attitude is at least part of the motivation behind all of the Maine books, but most particularly behind *Time of Wonder*. For this book is a celebration of the wonder and sheer beauty in the world off the coast of Maine. It is at the absolutely opposite extreme from the repetitive design of a suburban development. Instead, it celebrates the diversity and strangeness and color and sound and texture of the natural world.

Time of Wonder evokes the experiences of a single summer on an island off the coast of Maine, focusing principally on the experiences of two young girls. They watch as a rainstorm comes across the bay, sing as a fog lifts, and sail out into the open water at the height of the summer. When the tide is out, they play on the sun-warmed rocks and then, later, row over those same rocks at high tide. They batten down for a thunderstorm and go to sleep as the waves gently caress the rocks around the island. And when they leave the island, they are "a little bit sad about the place [they] are leaving, a little bit glad about the place [they] are going."[18]

This is the first book in which McCloskey used color to reproduce the natural world; he chose to use watercolor washes as the medium for his expression. This is especially effective in the skies he paints. They can be clear blue and marked by a thunderhead, misty blue to suggest a morning fog and then yellow as the fog is touched by the sun, dark blue and speckled with yellow stars, yellow then gray then black to portend a hurricane, pink and orange at the close of day. No sky has the same colors as the one before it, mirroring the ever-changing and unpredictable skies of New England.

This is true also of the ocean, which appears in many guises and reflects the constantly changing weather. It is true of the fauna of the Maine islands. There is the bright green of the young ferns, the darker green of the old pines, the sickly green of leaves under a yellow sky, the almost glowing green of moonlit trees. There is no machine-like repetition, no artificial, machine-generated color here. Instead, McCloskey uses color to show the wondrous design of the natural world he sees around him and to suggest the rhythms of life on an island. He himself attributed this new approach to May Massee and suggested that "it is her book, almost as surely as if she had held the brush in her hand."[19]

Three years in the making, the watercolor illustrations presented some difficulties in the final production process. Morris Colman wrote to McCloskey after some preliminary proofs to suggest changes that still had to be made to bring the final printing as close as possible to McCloskey's original drawings.

We have seen the lithographer come up to a pretty good reproduction from some pretty far-off first proofs, so I think we will find we are all right. . . .

The three fog subjects are much too heavy, and I have simply referred them back to the originals. . . .

The raindrop one was remade, and is closer in color, but they have made the rain streaks heavier (broader) than in your original, and I simply noted on the proof that I was going to check with you before telling them what needed to be done. . . .

The moon after storm is too bright, too contrasty, and weak in the blue. . . .

The children going up to bed: sky in window too warm, whole stairway and floor too light. . . .

Outdoor storm scene too contrasty, too sharp as compared with dimness and low key of original.[20]

Revisions were rapidly made and the book was published within four months of this letter.

In his Caldecott acceptance speech McCloskey spoke of the importance of spatial relationships in design, and it is clear from the first three pages of *Time of Wonder* that it is an important element in this book. He begins by placing the reader's perspective high over the island, so that the reader is on a level with the bottom of the thunderhead coming across Penobscot Bay (6–7). The island and the house backed against the pines are visible below, almost off the bottom of the page. But by the next illustration the perspective has come down a great deal, so that it is level with the tops of some of the islands in the distance (8–9). We are also much closer to McCloskey's own island, and Sal, Jane, and Penny are just visible on the point. By the third picture the perspective has come much closer, and it is focused on Sal and Jane and the rain beginning to come down on the point (10–11).

The cumulative effect of these three illustrations works in a number of ways. Most obviously it establishes the setting, the natural world within which everything will happen. It simulates the sensations that Sal and Jane experience as they watch the clouds scud across the bay, bringing the rain closer and closer until it begins to fall on them. And in a similar way, it brings the reader from the distant outside to a close participation in the life and experience of this family. The reader, along with the rain, comes to the island to experience a time of wonder.

This wonder is chiefly a product of the landscape, and the characters—particularly Sal and Jane—are always seen in relation to that landscape. They play beside age-old rocks, sing beside enormous pines, boat as porpoises frolic behind them and crabs scuttle below them, climb on a tree blown down by the hurricane. In one night scene they row across the bay; the islands in the background blend into each other and into the darkness of the night. The stars above them are mirrored in the water around them. They are seen as very small characters in the enormous—but gentle—natural world, a world in which "one pair of eyes is watching over all" (28).

As in *Blueberries for Sal* and *One Morning in Maine,* McCloskey evokes the wonder of the world by pointing out specific elements of the Maine shoreline. Porpoise feed on herring under the bay, the gulls and cormorants giggle "with their seabird sense of humor" (13) (an element that would be repeated in the giggling gull of *Burt Dow*), a mother seal nurses her baby by Swain's Cove Ledges, eider ducks and fishhawks and owls and herons watch at dusk. And there are the human activities associated with the New England shoreline. Harry Smith sails out to pull his lobster traps, sailboats race across Penobscot Bay at the summer's height, children swim off the point, Mr. Billings sights herring schools from his airplane, Clyde Snowman listens to the loons and predicts, with the unerring sense of the New England fisherman, that the storm will come soon, so boats are tied up "at Franky Day's boat yard up Benjamin River, and at Hal Vaughn's boat yard up Horseshoe Creek" (40). All of these elements—both natural and human—are elements of the Maine life that McCloskey and his family experienced and that he shares with the reader, bringing the reader into his world. "I tried to give a well-rounded impression of this island and to compress so much of our experiences here into those sixty-four pages," McCloskey was to say.[21]

To convey the world of the Maine coast McCloskey drew somewhat impressionistically; this represented a completely new approach to the illustration of children's books. He does not draw with the bold strong lines of *Blueberries for Sal* or the thinner, textured strokes of *One Morning in Maine*. His lines in *Time of Wonder* are much more subtle and depend more upon color than ever before. This is particularly true of the landscapes and the early morning fog, where objects have no distinct edges but are often mere impressions. The trees blend into each other, as opposed to their individual distinctiveness in *One Morning in Maine*. The characters are sketched in impressionistically; Sal and Jane here are drawn quite differently from their earlier appearances. And in the illustration of the children diving off the rock on the point of the island, McCloskey sketches in a child's pail, but only its barest outline can be seen, as though he had thought to draw it and abandoned it, but forgot to erase the lines (22). These illustrations mirror events that are recalled by McCloskey and filtered through the eye of the artist.

The impressionism of the illustrations is especially evident during the storm (44–45). No shape is really distinct here except for the square of yellow light that marks the house. The rest of the double-page spread is colored by streaks of blues and gray and violets and whites representing the wind-driven rains and seas. All is confusion on the outside of the house, but the next illustration shows the confusion that the storm brings to the inside as well (46–47). Gray and blue streaks again cross the page as the storm forces the door open and scatters lamps and books and parchesi games. The impression here suggests not only memory, but the chaos of the event.

Though the artwork is quite different from the earlier books, the matter of the story and the approach to the story are much the same. As with *Blueberries for Sal* and *One Morning in Maine,* McCloskey concentrates on the personal life of his family. Very little happens in terms of sheer plot; the reader is simply invited to participate in the slow rhythms of summer days. And yet, there is a real celebration of the ordinary world, which constantly suggests that apparently ordinary things are really quite extraordinary. The rock on the point is ages old, and was fiery hot at the beginning of the world and freezing cold when covered by a glacier. The castle built out of rocks of the beach during low tide is now the habitat of a crab which crawls beneath them as Sal and Jane coast in their rowboat at high tide. The sunflowers lift their heads yet again after being flattened by the storm. The girls find ancient shells under a storm-tossed tree; they crumble into dust at a touch. All of these are elements that evoke a time of wonder.

And when the family leaves the island at the end of the summer to resume the normal patterns of life on the mainland, McCloskey invokes a poignant leave-taking, and it is significant that the farewell is to a landscape. "Take a farewell look at the waves and sky. Take a farewell sniff of the salty sea. A little bit sad about the place you are leaving, a little bit glad about the place you are going. It is a time of quiet wonder—" (62). The landscape here becomes a metaphor for a way of life, and McCloskey looks back on it with some nostalgia as it passes away at the end of the season.

In addition to being a world of wonder, it is—as in most of McCloskey's work—a world of assurance and security. An island is itself, of course, an image of security. But throughout the book there is the presence of the affirming family. The greatest threat comes from the storm, but this is muted by the numerous warnings and the intense preparations. The family stocks up on gasoline and groceries, secures all the boats, brings in wood for a fire. And when the storm finally does hit, the constant yellow light that shines from their windows betokens the family's security against the hurricane. When the storm does break in for a moment, the father pushes the door and secures the house, tucking dishtowels by doorsills to keep the salt out. And arm in arm, the girls with their mother sing loudly to drown out the storm and read a familiar story.

And in the end the storm itself is subdued and becomes peaceful; the wind hums and sings chords against the trees as the girls go off to bed. The moon comes out and sheds its bright light in concentric rings. The waves foam over the point, and the wind lullabies the girls off to sleep. The world is secure again.

Many of the reviews noted that this was a book different from any other that McCloskey had yet written or illustrated. Frances Lander Spain noted that it was the first picture book done in color, though this was not quite accurate, since *Journey Cake, Ho!* had used multiple colors.[22] Ellen Lewis Buell in the *New York Times Book Review* perceived McCloskey's different handling of the narrator, moving from the child's perspective to that of the adult who observes the child.[23] And in *Horn Book* Jennie D. Lindquist wrote that "this is entirely different from any book he has done before" and suggested that the prose of the book was highly poetic.[24]

Both Buell and Lindquist touched on matters that dealt with the narrator of *Time of Wonder.* This is an entirely new perspective for McCloskey's narrator. It is an adult voice, a voice that has not lost the sense of wonder the child feels at the natural world. And at the same time it is a voice that details the child's perspective on the world. Though there is something of this in *Homer Price* and *Blueberries for Sal,* the stance is completely different here, for the narrator is speaking directly to the two young girls of the book.

Though theoretically it is not possible to have a narrator in the second person, McCloskey comes close to it here. "You hear a snorting sound from out of the nowhere and you know that no, you are not alone" (12), he writes. "In the afternoon you sail among the islands, pushed by gentle breezes" (20). On one level this is simply the narrator speaking directly to his characters. On another it is the author/artist Robert McCloskey speaking directly to his daughters and invoking a memory within them also. On yet another level this is McCloskey speaking directly to the reader, thus not only sharing the memory, but choosing a perspective that enables the reader to participate in the memory, to become, for a time, one of the family. This identification becomes so pronounced that at the end of the book, McCloskey tells his daughters and his readers, "It is the end of another summer. It is time for you to leave the island too (60)." Though the narrator seems to close off the identification of the reader with the characters on that same page—"And children, don't forget your toothbrushes"—he is actually continuing that identification by invoking a phrase most children have heard at some time. Similarly, the last line of the book asks the reader to wonder about the same thing as the characters: where *do* hummingbirds go in a hurricane?

The prose style in *Time of Wonder* is highly controlled, perhaps more than in any other of his books. At times he uses parallel structures to create suspense, as in the approaching clouds which move slowly over Penobscot Bay until "It's raining on *you!*" (10) and in the calm before the hurricane: "the incoming tide ripples past Eagle Island, ripples past Dirigo, past Pickering, past Two Bush Island. The bell-buoy off Spectacle Island sways slightly with the ripple, tolling . . ., tolling . . ., tolling the shift of the tide" (42). At times these same parallel structures are used to point out briefly or quickly a series of elements. Before the hurricane, "a mouse nibbles off one last stalk" and "a spider scurries across his web" (42). When they leave the island, the girls say goodbye to "clams and mussels and barnacles, to crows and swallows," and take "some gull feathers, a few shells, a book of pressed leaves" (60).

The prose is also highly poetic. From the time that the girls stand in the fog to the moment when the fog lifts, the prose becomes more and more like poetry, until finally it does indeed break into song. "You find that you are singing too, / With the blue water sparkling all around, all around, / With the blue water sparkling all around!" (18). Many other passages are marked by poetic techniques. There is the rhythm of "the bay is spotted with boats—with racing sailboats, with cruising schooners, with busy fishing boats, and with buzzing outboards" (20). There is the alliteration of "porpoises puffing and playing" (20), "a seal sniffs softly" (26), and "the gulls fly over, fussing and feuding" (30). There is the meter of "checking moorings, checking chains, checking pennants, getting ready" (34). The cadences and rhythms of the prose suggest the nostalgia of the narrator's memory, for even as the memories are filtered through the artist's eye, they are also filtered through the writer's hand.

But if McCloskey has chosen a different prose style, he has still maintained the same partite structure for his narrative. *Time of Wonder* is divided into five scenes: the rain coming over Penobscot Bay, the rising fog, the height of the summer season, preparations for the storm and its passing, preparations for leaving the island and the departure. The book begins and ends with the reader placed a great distance away from Sal and Jane, and each of the five sections concludes with Sal and Jane as central elements of the illustrations, as is appropriate since the reader is participating in the event and the reaction to it, and the narrator orients the reader so that he reacts in the same way that Sal and Jane react.

This is enhanced by the anonymity of the characters: though this is the McCloskey family, they are never named; they might be any children. And they might be living these experiences at any time. Since the book is written in the present tense, there is the sense that it deals with a memory constantly being relived as well as an ongoing event in the physical world.

> In the afternoon you sail among the islands, pushed by gentle breezes. You sail close by Swain's Cove Ledges, where a mother seal is nursing her baby.
>
> And then at sunset, with porpoises puffing and playing around your boat, you come about and set a course for the island that is home. (20)

This summer is a timeless one, a summer that is a constant in both memory and reality.

Most important, however, is that each section ends with a recognition of some marvelous element in the natural world: watching the rain coming gently toward you, feeling the lifting of the fog, sensing a supernatural providence in the expanse of the starry sky, understanding the continuity of life through finding the cache of shells. The accumulated effect—or the accumulated meaning—brings the reader to the same kinds of recognitions that the characters have come to, and perhaps that more than anything else is what is most significant and unique about the book.

Perhaps the events of the first three Maine books are not exactly factual; McCloskey recalls that Sally suggests that the world of Sal and Jane in the Maine books "is a never-never land that could never really be."[25] But the picture book is not meant merely to replicate reality; it is to mediate reality through the imagination of the artist. And that artist's vision informs the meaning of the book and gives the work its own imaginative reality that speaks to the child's experience.

Burt Dow, Deep-Water Man

The fourth Maine book, *Burt Dow, Deep-Water Man*, represented a movement away from chronicling the personal experiences of the McCloskey family and a movement back toward the tall-tale genre. This story, with its overtones of *Moby Dick* and the *Book of Jonah*, is still set in a bay, but it is an unnamed bay. None of the McCloskey family members appear. And though it begins with a realistic stance, it shortly moves into fantasy. Even its realism is laced with the implausible.

Yet at the same time this book is highly personal. The model for the character of Burt Dow did indeed live near McCloskey and was a family friend. He did have a boat "filled plumb to the gun'ls with earth,"[26] and he did plant it with vegetables each summer. When the dummy of the book was finished, McCloskey drove from New York to Maine and showed it to Bert Dow, who wrote "I like this story and you can use mine name for this sortey [sic]."[27] Later, McCloskey recalls, "Bert used to drop by occasionally to look over my shoulder and see what was happening, how they [the illustrations] were going along."[28]

Bert Dow did have a sister named Leela, and though she died before the final version of the book was published, Bert gave McCloskey permission to use her name. There was a Ginny Poor, though her pantry was not pink. Her husband was named Walton—McCloskey transformed him into Doc Walton—but his house trim was not green.

Bert did have a boat like the *Tidely-Idley*. McCloskey traded a gasoline engine for the boat and towed it over to his island on a scow because it would no longer sail.[29] It was indeed painted with many different colors and was held together with seal oil. It sat on the shore for two years before McCloskey began the book; he knew when he first traded for it that it would be the center of a story. For McCloskey, Bert Dow and his boats represented something classic—or archetypal—about a life close to the ocean, both in his way of life and in his language. (Sailing once with Bert, McCloskey recalls commenting on the large expanses of water. "'Nough water to float a dead man out there," Bert replied.)[30] He remained a close family friend until his death in 1986. His house has since been sold and torn down.

Though *Burt Dow, Deep-Water Man* does not deal directly with the McCloskey family, it does deal with their experience. The family is not immediately present, but behind the story is an artist's loving re-creation of a character, a boat, a way of life, a seascape. It is not a simple duplication of reality: there were no geraniums in the vegetable-laden dory, this detail coming from "front yards all up and down the coast of New England, planted with boatloads of begonias, geraniums, petunias, or you name it," as McCloskey recalls.[31] It is, as had been the case since *Lentil,* an artist's vision of that reality, a vision that orders details and events.

The story begins with the introduction of Burt Dow, his sister Leela, and Burt's two boats. The dory is drawn up on shore, filled with earth, and planted with geraniums and Indian peas. The *Tidely-Idley* is patched and painted with paint left over from odd jobs. Each morning Burt heads out into the bay accompanied by a giggling gull. There he fishes while recognizing that soon the *Tidely-Idley* would have to join the dory.

One morning he leaves the bay and heads out into the open sea. At first he catches nothing, and concludes that "there must be something down there frightening those fish" (21). He then hooks a whale's tail, and when the whale begins to slap water into the boat, Burt snips the barb off and puts a Band-Aid on the hole so that the blubber will not leak out. But "Burt had forgotten to keep his weather eyes out, what with getting this poor whale out of all the trouble he was in" (34) and finds that a storm has come upon him. The whale courteously swallows Burt and giggling gull to ride out the storm, but Burt fears that the whale might neglect to unswallow them.

Deciding to upset the whale's stomach, Burt coats it with old paint and sediment from the bottom of the boat: "it was the first time he'd ever had a chance really to express his personality in paint" (45). With a tickling of the gull's feathers, the whale belches them out, where they land in the middle of a school of whales, all of whom slap their tails at Burt. He soon discovers what they want, and they all line up to have their tails decorated with Band-Aids. After circling him they swim off. "'I never did see,' said Burt, 'so many tons of contentment come from out of such a little old band-aid box!'" (60). Burt and giggling gull head back up the bay. "They made it home just as the cock began to crow" (63).

The blend of fantasy and reality structures Burt's tale. Mc-Closkey had used some fantasy in earlier picture books; the anthropomorphic animals of *Make Way for Ducklings* and *Blueberries for Sal* are in some ways prototypes for the whale and giggling gull, who are also slightly anthropomorphized. But this is the first picture book that might truly be called a tall tale. And like many tall tales, it begins in reality, as the story of Pecos Bill begins with a family heading out west to find a place to settle, or the tale of Johnny Appleseed begins with Johnny heading across the Appalachians to plant apples. After being introduced to the reader, Burt too takes a journey, his leading beyond the end of the bay.

Here, outside of the bound world of the bay, is a place of infinite potential, and soon the implausible happens: Burt hooks a whale's tail. From here on, each episode is increasingly fantastic in scope: Burt gives the whale a Band-Aid; the whale swallows Burt; Burt escapes by coating the whale's stomach with sediment; Burt is surrounded by a school of whales demanding Band-Aids. Only in the final page is the fantasy dispelled; the whales have swum off, and there is no mention of them in the text. Instead, Burt and giggling gull head back up into the bay and make it home at dawn.

From the time he begins fishing to his waking at dawn, "my feeling is that Burt Dow is dreaming a dream," McCloskey has remarked.[32] This would explain, in a realistic setting, the tall tale itself, the expressionistic paintings of the whales, which are really extensions of Burt's painting inside the whale, and the time sequence of the book, since it would seem that the nighttime hours are missing. In any case, the boundary between reality and fantasy is a seamless one in *Burt Dow* so that neither Burt nor the reader is aware of any distinctions between the two.

Certainly *Burt Dow* has all the elements of the tall tale: the impossible situations, the unflappable protagonist, the implausible made to seem everyday. However, the story also tends to debunk the high seriousness of epic tales it recalls. Here, Moby Dick is hooked and turns out to be a rather obliging, childlike fellow who is completely inoffensive. And here, Jonah is swallowed by his own wish and finds a place of safety inside the whale. Like Jonah, Burt comes to certain realizations about himself, but these do not lead to penitential prayers; they lead to expressionistic art: "it was the first time he'd ever had a chance to express his personality in paint" (45). McCloskey never allows *Burt Dow* to take on the serious tone of any of these earlier tales. The tone is one of understated humor, deriving both from the impossible situations of the tall-tale genre and peripheral elements from Leela's boisterous mastery, giggling gull's bemused reactions, and Burt's unlikely painting style.

At the same time *Burt Dow, Deep-Water Man* is subtitled *A Tale of the Sea in the Classic Tradition*. Although this refers in part to the epic tales, it refers more strongly to McCloskey's playful use of clichéd situations and language from classic sea tales. The whale hunt itself is an element of such tales, though here it is inverted. Similarly the threatening sea storm and peaceful dawn recall sea tales. The most prominent element of the classic sea tradition is Burt's language. "'Ahoy there, whale!' bellowed Burt . . . 'Head into the wind and slack off the main sheet!'" (28). When the whale slaps his tail, Burt cries, "He's about to stave us in and send the *Tidely-Idley* and all hands straight to Davy Jones's locker!" (29), a line he repeats when the storm comes close to sinking the boat. Later, when the whales circle him, spouting, "An old deep-water man like Burt couldn't resist shouting, 'Thar she blows!' in the best classic tradition" (59).

McCloskey plays even with this definition of classic, as though refusing to allow things to get even this serious, for this is, after all, a dream. So when Burt asks to be swallowed, the whale "opened his mouth wide and said, 'AH-H-H!'—in the classic tradition" (37). And when Burt is burped out into the school of whales, he remarks, "'Well!!! That's a whale of a lot of whale tails'—making what amounted to a classic understatement" (51). The result is that the classic tale is both evoked and undercut at the same moment.

The complexity of the classicism of the tale suggests that this narrator is further distanced from the action than the narrators of the three other Maine books. The narrator announces to the reader that he is taking a specific stance. After introducing Burt, his boats, his sister, and his pet, McCloskey begins the actual tale with a line similar to that which begins *One Morning in Maine*: "One morning the cock crowed . . ." (16). The storyteller is absolutely separate from the subject—an enormous change from the interrelatedness of narrator and character in *One Morning in Maine* and *Time of Wonder*.

Despite this separation, the narrator's language indicates a sensibility that is close to that of Burt Dow. The narrator too speaks with the voice of the New England coast: "Burt Dow's dory is filled plumb to the gun'ls with earth . . . The geraniums brighten up the deck, and the Indian peas climb the rigging and sway this-a-way, that-a-way, in a smoky sou'wester" (7). When Burt pulls up the whale's tail, the narrator interjects, "Or 'twas t'other-way-round—the tail of a whale had pulled up *Burt*! . . . Burt finally slacked up on the line, or 'twas t'other-way-round— finally the *tail* slacked up on the line. But then the tail began to thrash about, this-a-way, that-a-way" (27). When Burt calls to the whale, the narrator notes that "the whale couldn't hear because his hearing gear was so far upwind from his steering gear that had come afoul of Burt's cod hook" (28).

The narrator's language is very similar to Burt's, though he does not use some of the clichés that Burt strings together. The use of nautical phraseology, the clipped articles and pronouns, the idioms, the phrases made parallel by idiomatic diction—all evoke the language of an old New England deep-water man. It is not surprising then that at times the narrator and the character seem to work in tandem, where the narrator will make a comment that is immediately backed up by Burt, as though the character breaks into the narrative. "Leela is a very impatient person—" the narrator notes, and "'Most impatient being on land or sea,' says Burt" (10). "Burt kept studying the color of the sky, the color of the water, and the direction of the wind," recounts the narrator. And the next line includes Burt's agreement: "'An old deep-water man like me always keeps a weather eye out,' says Burt" (17–18).

The present-tense "says" suggests that these comments are typical of ones that Burt has made in the past, and that here he is expressing long-held sentiments. But the tense also suggests a present interaction with the narrator, so that the reader is being told a story in the immediate present by an unnamed narrator and by Burt himself, who seems aware of the presence of the reader. Though this awareness is expressed throughout the text, it comes in only one illustration: when Burt first feels the whale on his line, he looks out at the reader, his face registering surprise and some wonder (22).

Most of Burt's comments—made principally to giggling gull— seem to be interjections into the narrator's telling of the tale. While his language mirrors that of the narrator, Burt's voice is much more flexible, for while the narrator maintains the consistent stance of one who is telling a story, Burt is the character engaged in the story, and so his voice will necessarily be affected by events. His voice is saddened as he thinks of the time when the *Tidely-Idley* will no longer float; calm and controlled when confronted by the storm; chuckling as he creates abstract art; content as he decks the whales with band-aids. Burt's voice consistently responds to the plot situation.

Cuts from a late dummy suggest McCloskey's conscious recognition of the importance of Burt's voice and its consistency. One such cut occurred on the two black pages that show Burt's predicament inside the whale:

> "We've got to make certain, giggling gull," Burt said solemnly, "that we get regurgitated!" Then he tried to strike a few more matches and light the lantern. "Can't leave a word like regurgitated in the dark—some authority is apt to stumble over it, bark his shins, and blame us 'cause it isn't on the right word list."[33]

Another deleted passage comes on the page where Burt is heading home:

> Then Burt noticed that the sky had turned pink—the color of Ginny Poor's pantry.
> "Perplexing, how that identical pink keeps popping up on these pages," Burt mumbled to himself, "I think it must be pink ink they printed 'em with."

Both of these metafictive passages would have hurt the continuity of the story by dramatically shifting Burt's point of view. His comments on vocabulary and printing distance him further from the action than even the narrator, and would have established a distinctly different relationship with the reader, one that broke the semblance of reality that is important as the frame for the whale incident.

As these two voices mesh to tell the story, they manipulate sound in a playful manner, sometimes using sound to suggest reality. The rooster crows "cockety-doodly"; Leela rattles her stove "klinkety-klink"; the pump sounds "slish-cashlosh, slish-cashlosh"; the make-and-break engine runs "clackety bang, clackety bang." The alliteration and consonance of these coupled words create a sense of realism at the same time that they create pleasing aural effects; that is, at the same time that they participate in the telling of the story.

Many of these sounds are repeated throughout the tale, recurring reference points rooted in reality during the fantastic adventures. Leela's insistent commands; the references to the pink of Ginny Poor's pantry and the green of Doc Walton's waiting room; the images of Burt, "firm hand on the tiller, giggling gull flying along behind"; the water coming up over the floorboards—all of these images are repeated again and again. On one level this represents a narrator telling a story in the tall-tale tradition. On another, it represents a way of structuring Burt's experience through language.

Burt's experience is also told through color. In *Time of Wonder* McCloskey had used color to evoke setting. In *Burt Dow, Deep-Water Man* it is used much more prominently in the storyline itself. The opening pages—painted in the brightest, most vivid colors McCloskey had ever used in his books—announce the importance of color. "One dory is so old and so leaky that it can no longer be launched. Burt has painted it red and placed it on the little patch of lawn in front of his house, overlooking the bay" (6). The accompanying illustration uses all of the colors evoked by these images, adding the blue tones of the sea and sky, the bright white of the house and hens, the yellow of Burt's slicker and the chicks, the greens of the Indian peas, geranium leaves, and the lawn.

Color also plays an important part in moving the plot along. This is especially evident after Burt has hooked the whale. While Burt is fishing, McCloskey uses a white sky behind the boat. From the moment that the whale's full tail shows, the sky gets grayer and grayer; the seas get greener and darker. Neither Burt nor the reader notices this immediately; both simultaneously recognize that the storm has crept up on them. In contrast, the two black pages appear suddenly and strikingly, as both the reader and Burt travel inside the whale.

In the same way that McCloskey repeats phrases, he repeats a single color motif. The title page pictures giggling gull walking through a puddle of pink paint and leaving his footprints across the page. Behind the puddle is an open gallon of green paint. (Presumably these are the paint cans from Ginny Poor's pantry and

Doc Walton's waiting room.) These two colors, chosen because they clash so stridently, appear throughout the book.[34] In the old dory they appear in the pink geraniums against the green Indian peas. In the *Tidely-Idley* they appear in adjacent planks. In the grouping of townspeople they appear in the upturned boat on the lawn (14–15). As Burt is swallowed, they appear in the green water foaming against the whale's open mouth. And the colors appear in a number of different tones in the circle of whales demanding band-aids. The resolution of this clash comes in the final page, as Burt heads home. Here the greens and pinks have been considerably softened into pastel shades. They no longer conflict but together suggest a tone of peaceful harmony.

The colors of this final page also represent a return to realism. As Burt moves further into the fantastic part of his journey, the colors become more and more vivid. The black pages yield to a bright expressionist painting. This itself yields to an extraordinary collection of expressionist whales. These pink and green and rust and purple and brown behemoths are, in some ways, further expressions of Burt's personality. His interest in color as seen in the *Tidely-Idley* is, in a dream context, given fuller expression.

In the end, the book is not only about Burt's experience with the whales; it is, perhaps, more about Burt's way of life which is now coming to a close. It is about a calm, assured, enduring character who lives in close conjunction with the natural world; in this guise, Burt is not particularly different from the characters in the three other Maine books. He too exists in a bound world—the *Tidely-Idley*, and the strain of sadness that runs underneath the storyline is connected to the future loss of that bound world. As in *Blueberries for Sal, One Morning in Maine,* and *Time of Wonder,* the protagonists of *Burt Dow* return home at the end of the story, but for Burt it is neither a gentle nor an easy homecoming.

6

Late Collaboration:
Focusing the Reader's Eye

McCloskey's six final collaborative works spanned almost two decades and dealt with a variety of subjects: a folktale set in Appalachia, an Airedale acclimating an urban family to the country, and a young boy whose escapades recall those of Homer Price. Though the subjects are widely different, they are linked by McCloskey's manipulation of the reader's angle of perception. In all six works the illustrations place the reader in a position from which plot situations and characters can be observed and judged. This concern dominates the illustrations of all these books and points to a growth in McCloskey's vision of the role of the collaborative illustrator.

Journey Cake, Ho!

In 1953 McCloskey illustrated a folktale set in the mountains of Appalachia, *Journey Cake, Ho!* The text was by Ruth Sawyer, a prominent writer of children's literature and McCloskey's mother-in-law. She designed the work to be a recitative piece, something like Sergey Prokofiev's *Peter and the Wolf* had been. Isadore Freed composed the music, intending the completed work to be a children's opera. Funded by the Hartt School of Music in Hartford,

Connecticut, a number of the songs were eventually recorded, though the full orchestration for the piece was not. However, the musical aspect of the project was never completed; instead, Ruth Sawyer believed that the story could be made into a picture book (by this time Warren Chappell had illustrated *Peter and the Wolf*). Today only the book itself stands as the finished project.

Nevertheless, the book fairly dances with the music that is in it. The text, while not poetic, seems always to be about to break into poetry. The characters—both human and animal—seem to step in a highly choreographed dance across a stage. Even the journey cake itself sings, though tauntingly: "Journey Cake, ho! / Journey Cake, hi! / Catch me and eat me / As I roll by!"[1]

The story opens with an introduction of the old man and woman and their young hired boy, Johnny. The narrator suggests that "nothing happened for a long, long time. They lived snug, like rabbits in their burrow" (15). But then a fox kills the hens, a wolf carries off the sheep, the pig wanders off, and the cow breaks her leg. Faced with scant resources, the couple concludes that "what will feed two will not feed three" (20). Reluctantly, they send the boy away.

In the morning Johnny departs with a journey cake strapped to his back to seek a new master and ma'am. But soon the cake breaks off and rolls free; Johnny rushes after it. As the cake taunts him, Johnny is joined in his chase by a brindle cow, a white duck, a white and black sheep, a spotted pig, a flock of red hens, and a gray donkey. Each seeks to eat the cake, but it eludes them all. Finally, as the cake heads uphill, it goes slower and slower; the pursuers all slow down, and finally they spiral to a halt back at the farm that Johnny had left. There, Johnny gives the animals to the couple, who are now better off than they ever had been. They celebrate by sharing the journey cake, now called a Johnny cake.

Journey Cake, Ho! is a folktale, a variant of the European gingerbread boy tale. (It was the last of the genre that McCloskey was to work with. Though the story of Burt Dow might be properly called a tall tale, it does not come out of an oral tradition like the other tall tales McCloskey had illustrated.) The story is a cu-

mulative one, as one disaster after another comes upon the el-
derly farm couple, and then one animal after another chases after
the journey cake. In this structure the tale resembles McCloskey's
partite patterning of his own texts, as the book clearly divides
itself into two separate events: the opening disasters and the
frantic chase with its resolution.

McCloskey's opening illustrations introduce the characters as
though they are on a stage. In the first double-page spread all
three principal characters appear, looking directly at the reader;
they seem to comment about their world to the reader. Each of
these portraits establishes dominant traits for the characters: the
old woman, Merry, with her kitchen utensils and broad smile; the
old man, Grumble, leaning on a hoe with a dispirited frown;
Johnny striding away with his pail, whistling as he heads toward
his chores. And indeed, these portraits are further defined in the
next three spreads. Merry virtually dances with glee as she sings
and bakes the journey cake. Grumble scratches at the earth with
his hoe as he complains about life: "A bother, a pest! / All work
and no rest! / Come winter, come spring, / Life's a nettlesome
thing" (11). But Johnny whistles happily as the animals gather
around to eat. His whistling suggests a general contentedness
that recalls the music-making of both Lentil and Homer.

If McCloskey has presented these characters as though they
were on a stage, then the land itself is that stage, as suggested
by the next spread. Here McCloskey pictures the entire hilltop.
Crowned by a ring of sharply defined evergreens, the hill is gir-
dled by a road that winds down into the valley. The small farm
and its livestock straddle the road. As Sawyer writes, "Their
whole world lay close about them. There were the garden patch,
the brook, the logging road that ran down to the valley where the
villagers lived, and the spruce woods" (14). The effect of the illustration—and the text—is to suggest a complete and isolated
world, recalling the bound worlds of McCloskey's own texts. This
makes the coming disasters appear all the more dreadful, for
there is no communal support. Even the one community of the
book—that between Merry, Grumble, and their bound-out boy—
is broken by the loss of the farm animals.

The reader is never unaware of the rolling Appalachian terrain. Aside from providing a natural background to the illustrations, it paces the chase for the journey cake. As the cake rolls into the valley, it eludes its pursuers by its sheer momentum and speed. McCloskey illustrates the breathlessness of its chant—"Journey Cake, ho! / Journey Cake, hi! / Catch me and eat me / As I roll by!" (20)—by suggesting the cake's rapid rotation and elongating its shape. Later the cake rolls up the mountain, and as it slows, its chant begins to falter: "C-c-catch me and eat me— / As I roll along" (37). McCloskey slows the rotation and rounds out the cake, and soon it reaches the top of the mountain where it flops down. The landscape has shaped the chase itself so that they are all back where they started.

The natural world is also very participatory in *Journey Cake, Ho!* Most noticeable are the animals that enter into the chase; when they are led to the farm, they happily enter a world of domestic security with expressions of high contentedness. This atones for the sorrow at Johnny's leaving, a sorrow that is expressed in the flowers that wilt at his departure. Raucus the crow also reacts to events, but his reactions bridge the gap between the story and its reader.

Though Raucus plays only a minor role in the text, he is given an important role in the illustrations. He is placed at the top of the tallest tree; when he is first shown, he is disproportionately large. Later, the crow dominates an entire page on two different spreads, and the reader looks down from the crow's high perspective. Like the reader, Raucus seems to be distanced from the activities played out before him. But also like the reader, the crow is pulled into those activities and becomes so involved that he cannot help but react to them. When the pig wanders off and the cow breaks her leg, Raucus caws all day in a lament as pitiful as that of the poor farmers. When the new animals arrive, McCloskey again perches the reader with Raucus, suggesting the impossibility of any distancing.

The drawings for *Journey Cake, Ho!* are heavily stylized, more stylized than any other McCloskey illustrations for children's books. McCloskey uses great blocks of teal blue to suggest things as different as a pasture, an evergreen, a log cabin, and Johnny's britches. A dark shading is used to vary the texture between these, as it is used to suggest shadows in the single night scene. The stark white road stands out in dramatic contrast to this, as do the blackened evergreens and the stark white trees. Throughout the book McCloskey does not try to simulate real natural features, as he does in *Blueberries for Sal* or *One Morning in Maine*. Instead, he evokes a natural terrain by suggesting shape and texture, a technique often used in primitive folk art, and thus a technique appropriate to this folktale.

The terrain itself reflects the stylized technique. Uninterested in verisimilitude, McCloskey uses his striking colors for effects and is not committed to a faithful reproduction of a setting. The result is that the farm takes on several different guises. Sometimes the road runs directly in front of it and down the valley (14–15); sometimes the road runs around and behind the cabin (18–19); sometimes it runs in front of and away from the cabin (38–39); and sometimes it is not near the cabin at all (40–41). This is not another example of the fifth robber in *Homer Price*. It is instead a willingness to manipulate illustrations for specific purposes. One road placement suggests the circular hill and isolation of the farm (14–15); another is placed to define the landscape behind Raucus (18–19); another emphasizes the spiraling chase (38–39); and its absence is necessary to suggest the reunion of the three characters (40–41). Such manipulation can be done in these heavily stylized drawings, whereas it could not be done in the illustrations of a book like *Make Way for Ducklings,* which depends so much on realism.

The characters themselves are also stylized; this is seen particularly in their postures and gestures. Each of the characters is marked by a distinct angularity. The final illustration culminates these angled postures with squared shoulders, elbows, and legs, as though the characters were in an elaborate dance calling for such steps. Johnny in particular is placed in dramatic postures; he never stands still or straight. During the chase sequence his feet never touch the ground and his chest leans impossibly far in front of his feet.

The effect of these stylized postures is to invest these illustrations with intense energy. Johnny's frenetic pursuit of the journey cake lends an impetus to that of the other animals. The galloping of these animals later leads to an easy stroll to their various shelters. The final dance-like celebration of the three human characters contrasts to their prone stillness in the face of disaster. The ending is exuberant, made more so by the sense of movement suggested by the stylized illustrations.

This conclusion suggests a certain linear growth—Grumble is now a happy man and dances with Johnny and Merry—but it also suggests a kind of circling: things are back to the way they were at the beginning, and all three have come to value their situation more. (This is a variant from the traditional folktale where the cake is eaten by a character ostensibly saving the cake from its pursuers.) This circling is the dominant motif of the book, both in terms of the text and the illustrations. In the tale circumstances move the characters through cycles of depression and elation. In addition, Johnny's journey takes him around a valley and back up to his original starting place.

McCloskey's illustrations reflect this motif, so that there is hardly a single spread that does not use a circle in some way. This appears most often in the oddly circular clouds, which are drawn as bands of white; they suggest the path that Johnny takes. Though the reader never sees the complete path, it is clear that the white path is, like the cloud, a circle. These circles appear in smaller details as well: the journey cake itself and its spiraling, the motif on Merry's bandanna, the pails and frypans, the wide brimmed hats, the moon, the spots on a pig, the bold circles on the stumps the chickens roost on, the circle formed around Johnny by the cow's neck, chest, and foreleg and a duck's back as they all chase the cake (37), the spiraling procession of animals as the journey cake slows and flops on its side.

Certainly this motif foreshadows and reflects the circular journey that Johnny will take. But it also is a source of great hope in this book, for it suggests that everything will come out right in the end—as indeed it does. None of McCloskey's later work will use a motif in quite this single-minded way again. What will appear again, though, is an emphasis on the role of a landscape in affecting the meaning of a story.

Junket, the Dog Who Liked Everything "Just So"

Journey Cake, Ho! was the last picture book that McCloskey was to collaborate on; his last five collaborative works were all novels: Anne White's *Junket* and Keith Robertson's Henry Reed series. McCloskey's illustrations for these novels—particularly *Junket* and *Henry Reed, Inc.*—are much more interpretive than those he did for earlier collaborative work. Unwilling merely to decorate, McCloskey used his illustrations to interpret the story and to add to it, much as an illustrator would do in a picture book.

In *Junket, the Dog Who Liked Everything "Just So"* McCloskey found a text that would allow him to illustrate from a dog's eye view. The story itself focuses primarily on the consciousness of Junket, a roaming Airedale who lives in the country and takes his meaning from the chores he does each day. Most of the events in the text are perceived from the dog's perspective, so that the reader judges and evaluates characters in the same way that Junket evaluates them.

In the story Junket arrives one afternoon at the Jellicot farm (the Jellicots are his nominal owners) to find that they have sold the farm and given away the animals; the McDonegal family has moved in. Mr. McDonegal, unaware of the beauty and reality of the world around him, immerses himself in the classics. Mrs. McDonegal spends her hours searching for Agreeable Subjects for her paintings. The children pine for animals. And Junket laments the upsetting of his daily routine; everything is not "just so."[2] The rest of the novel chronicles how Junket reestablishes the past by educating the McDonegals, teaching them how to live in the country.

Reviews of *Junket* lauded both the story and the illustrations. "Robert McCloskey's black-and-white illustrations have the same wonderful humor as Mrs. White's story," wrote Frances Lander Spain in the *Saturday Review*.[3] Marjorie Fisher in the *New York*

Times Book Review suggested "this is a light-hearted, amusing story, brilliantly illustrated by Robert McCloskey."[4] And Katherine Kinkead in the *New Yorker* called Junket "a comical tale, which is expertly told and zestfully illustrated with black-and-white drawings."[5] Though enthusiastic, none of these reviewers explored how the illustrations worked with the text.

One reason for the success of these illustrations is the tale itself, which contains several themes and motifs that McCloskey used in his own stories. Included here is a celebration of the natural landscape as opposed to an urban landscape, and the gradual incorporation of a family into the natural world. The adult characters are comically exaggerated; the child characters have episodic adventures that lead to a conversion of adult attitudes. Each of the animals, particularly Junket, is personified while at the same time a consistent animal nature is maintained. McCloskey would pick up on all of these elements in his illustrations.

As with many of his illustrations, these present figures who are slightly caricatured: the prim, straight-backed Mr. McDonegal, and the silly, absurd Mrs. McDonegal are characterized as much by the illustrations as by the text. Often characters are caught in the middle of an expression, so that their surprise or irritation or stubbornness or pride seem to be physically manifested. McCloskey, always interested in the ordinary as well as the extraordinary, uses the normal elements of everyday life in the country to generate the kind of humor that the text itself has: a gentle undercutting of pride and stubbornness. The three children are weighed down with garden tools; their stance suggests to the reader that they are unlikely to succeed in establishing a vegetable garden (49). Mrs. McDonegal is entranced by a pig who ignores her existence (118). Mr. McDonegal stumbles over a cow (170) and is trapped against a fence by a horse (173).

All of these illustrations are derived from the text itself; all humorously portray the McDonegals' confrontation with country life. Still other illustrations add to the text by creating plot situations not in the text: Junket appears under a breakfast table to defy the strict dictum of "No Animals!" (68–69). Others establish the landscape; this is seen particularly in the walks that Junket takes with Montgomery (94–95) and Mrs. McDonegal (116–17). Other illustrations contribute to characterization: a still life with a smoking toaster, teacup, and scattered paints and brushes suggests Mrs. McDonegal's abstracted life (111). Several illustrations combine planes of action to present a sequence of events simultaneously. In one, Mr. McDonegal poses angrily for his wife, who is calmly beginning her picture. Junket bounds into the scene behind her (Mr. McDonegal must surely see the dog, but he gives no indication of this); the three children are dismayed and surprised (44–45). A later illustration shows Margaret atop her horse. In front of her, each parent presents a strikingly different reaction (80–81). Bringing together these consecutive events into one picture gives the illustration enormous energy, as well as bringing the events closer to real life, where events do not always occur in the set sequences suggested by a narrative storyline.

The variety of purposes to which McCloskey puts his illustrations and his artistic interpretations of characters and events make this work his most interesting collaboration on a novel. One additional reason for this judgment, though, is McCloskey's use of Junket himself. Though the novel uses a third-person narrator, much of the action is seen from the perspective of Junket. Often the narrator enters into the consciousness of the Airedale, who is engaged with getting his world back "just so." The result is that many of the illustrations present a dog's-eye view. This is different from the duck's-eye view of *Make Way for Ducklings,* where the illustrations force the reader to look at scenes from a duck's perspective. Instead, these illustrations force the reader to evaluate situations in the same way that Junket evaluates them.

So Junket romps among the three children with a completely self-satisfied expression, as though this were absolutely proper for a dog to do (28–29). He bounds into a painting session, his excitement suggesting the silliness of the scene (44–45). He looks listlessly out from the garden, seemingly criticizing forced work (89). He carries a squalling baby as though it were a most unpleasant bundle (102). He walks proudly with the family on the way to the fair (154–155). And the dog looks critically at Mr.

McDonegal when he fails to understand the need for animals in a country setting (167). In each case, the reader tends to agree with Junket's implied assessments. To the Airedale, the Mc-Donegals are rather silly people who need to be taught how to live in the country; Junket's judgments as indicated in the illustrations all work toward this education.

The illustrations of Junket's judgments are particularly striking in that the judgments are often made in the context of an intimate relationship established between the reader and Junket. At times Junket turns away from the world of the narrative to look directly at the reader, establishing a relationship with the reader that the characters do not have. McCloskey had used this same technique in *Trigger John's Son,* but not as successfully. In the earlier novel Trigger had smiled benignly out of the pages at the reader; Junket's expressions are much more complex.

The frontispiece for *Junket* shows a barnyard scene. The pictured animals suggest that this is a scene that is "just so"—just as Junket would have it be. The dog himself leans out from one of the doors, beckoning to the reader, as though inviting the reader into this properly organized world. The repetition of this scene at the end of the novel suggests that all is as it was before. The first illustration of Junket that accompanies the text works similarly (11). Junket is walking with a sprightly step. Pictured against the background of the old farm, he looks out at the reader as though to imply that things are exactly as they should be. His proud stance lends him an air of importance, befitting the opening lines of the novel: "This is the story of a dog named Junket, who knew how to live in the country, and it is the story of a family who did not know how until Junket taught them. Junket was a very large and very busy Airedale" (11).

The concluding illustration again establishes a link between Junket and the reader. When Montgomery, one of the McDonegal children, observes that everything will be just so again once the farm again has animals, the narrator notes that "Junket yawned. That was no news to him. What did they think he had been working for all summer?" (184). The illustration shows Junket looking back over his shoulder at the reader. His expression suggests that his success at bringing back the animals should have been obvious to the reader, as well as to the characters. The book closes with the illustration of a very self-assured dog.

There is a close unity of story and illustrations in *Junket*. Both rely on gentle humor. Both focus on Junket as the mediator of that humor for the reader. Both story and pictures have a similar stance toward all of the characters, but at the same time the illustrations extend the tale and develop narrative relationships that the text does not establish. While this is perhaps common in picture books, it is not so common in illustrations for novels. In fact, few of the illustrations for the Henry Reed series would be so complex.

The Henry Reed Series

After *Time of Wonder* May Massee asked McCloskey to illustrate Keith Robertson's *Henry Reed, Inc.* Henry Reed was the last in a line of boy protagonists that McCloskey would illustrate. He has some of the physical characteristics of Tom Robinson's Trigger and the love of small-town adventure of Homer Price. And all three—Trigger, Homer, and Henry—are interested to some extent in the natural world, gadgets, and the circumvention of the adult world.

But Henry Reed is different in kind from these other figures. Intensely literal-minded, he lacks Homer's imaginative capacities; he seems almost unable to assess his own participation in the adventures he instigates. His comments about himself and other characters are often ironically undercutting, suggesting a kind of introspection that would have been foreign to Trigger and Homer. He seems half-unaware, almost naive at times, despite his general amiability, inventiveness, and good sense.

Each of the five Henry Reed books is presented as a journal, so that Henry himself recounts his adventures in Grover's Corner, New Jersey. The journal form requires an introspective narrator, and also raises the possibility of an unreliable narrator, one who is uncertain about the meaning of events. To some extent this is true of Henry; though he grows older in the novels, he never grows wiser.

This leads to a significant problem for an illustrator. The humor and interest of the books lie not only in the plot situations, but especially in the interplay between Henry's account and the reader's evaluation of his perspective. While illustrations could exploit the humor of the text, they would also need to participate in the complex narrative relationship that is so important to the books. Perhaps the only way this might have been done is by creating the impression of a first-person illustration; that is, by having the reader look through Henry's eyes, having the reader perceive the same skewed vision of the world that Henry sees.

This is precisely what McCloskey does in a number of his illustrations, and here he is most successful in these books. He often pictures Henry as an observer to odd goings-on, so that Henry seems the one center of normalcy in a scene of crazed or exaggerated situations. And this mirrors Henry's own stance in his journal.

At times McCloskey draws back from this perspective to a more conventional one, where the reader shares with the illustrator a removed, perhaps more objective vision of Henry Reed and his adventures. Such illustrations often introduce characters, establish landscapes, or simply present humorous plot details. Most of the books begin with a picture of Henry Reed, mirroring the opening of the journals. The claim "My name is Henry Harris Reed and this is my journal" opens both *Henry Reed, Inc.* (7) and *Henry Reed's Journey* (9). These assertions establish the need for a opening illustration that identifies Henry, and no more than five pages go by before such an establishing illustration appears.

Though none of the illustrations for the Henry Reed books significantly add to the plot or the novels' meanings, and though they do not have the artistic complexity of those for *Johnny Cake, Ho!* or the flexibility of purpose of those for *Junket,* they do work to establish character. Keith Robertson said that McCloskey was the only illustrator who drew a character as he had imagined he should look.[6] Certainly Henry—and Midge and Uncle Al and Agony and the rest of the characters—match the details presented in the text. But the illustrations also convey character: Henry's deep interest in the natural world, Midge's excessive enthusiasm, Uncle Al's humorous vision of his nephew. The result is that the reader would find it difficult to dissociate the illustrations from the texts: McCloskey's vision of the characters has united with Robertson's.

So it is not surprising that when Robertson wrote *Henry Reed's Think Tank,* he and Regina Hayes, the current children's book editor at Viking Press, asked McCloskey to illustrate the book. "Of course after the first Henry Reed book, I would have objected strenuously had Viking wanted to use another illustrator,"[7] Robertson has noted. McCloskey did not take on the project, and in 1986 the book was published—with no illustrations.

Henry Reed, Inc. introduces the series. The son of a diplomat, Henry lives with his parents in Naples and Manila for most of the year, with his uncle and aunt in Grover's Corner, New Jersey, for the summer. While in Grover's Corner he embarks on a series of adventures all under the auspices of his research institute. Accompanied by Midge, he does such things as sell fishing worms, chase rabbits, drill for oil, douse for water, paint and sell turtles, hunt for truffles, and test hot air balloons. Each enterprise soon becomes entangled in a series of comic misadventures, leading Uncle Al to conclude that Henry, like his mother before him, tends to be a focal point for disaster.

McCloskey uses fewer illustrations for this novel than for *Junket,* perhaps because *Henry Reed, Inc.* is for a slightly older audience. As the series progressed, he used fewer and fewer illustrations. Part of the reason for this decrease is that toward the end of the series, McCloskey became dissatisfied with the look and feel of the book, noting that the final book "looked like it came out of a Xerox machine."[8] Another reason for the decrease is the need to avoid repetition: Grover's Corner, the setting for three of the four books that McCloskey illustrated, is depicted as a very small town (ten houses), so the possibilities are somewhat limited. The cast of characters is also limited, Midge and Henry being the most prominent subjects.

In *Henry Reed, Inc.,* however, everything is new and there is a

wide range of material to illustrate. As with his other books, much of McCloskey's humor comes through the expressions and poses of his characters. The fine lines of his brush-and-ink pictures particularly lend themselves to facial detail, and McCloskey will often manipulate this to accord with the humor in the text. The expression that is the least changeable is that of Henry Reed himself; since he is recalling the story after the event and the illustrations arise, presumably, from his retelling, the constancy of expression is appropriate.

Since Henry is a witness to all that goes on, a number of the illustrations picture him as that witness: the reader watches Henry watching something, and draws conclusions from the text and the illustration about Henry's reaction to what he is watching. An early illustration of Henry climbing into bed while watching his newly acquired beagle is marred by a missing detail (the dog should be curled up on a rag rug, though he may not have shown up as well as he does on the plank floor), but it suggests Henry's fondness for animals, his quick devotion to Agony, and his sense of the appropriateness of a boy having a dog curled at the foot of his bed (26).[9]

The effect of this and other illustrations where Henry acts as a witness is to draw the reader closer to Henry's perspective, so that the reader becomes involved in the same misadventures that fall upon Henry and Midge. In addition, such illustrations stress Henry's intensely inquisitive nature: he is always handling some tool, searching out some reaction, investigating some intriguing possibility.

Published five years later, the plot of *Henry Reed's Journey* begins one year after that of *Henry Reed, Inc.* Henry has traveled to San Francisco, where he has met Midge's family; he accompanies them back across the United States to their home in Grover's Corner. Traveling through the Southwest, Henry and Midge visit Yosemite National Park, Los Angeles, Las Vegas, the Grand Canyon, New Mexico, Colorado, and Kansas before they drive back to New Jersey. Along the way various adventures befall them: they start a gold rush, are adopted by Hopi Indians, fall off a boat in Disneyland, and set off a barrage of fireworks.

Henry is a year older now, so McCloskey has aged the character in his illustrations. Over the course of the four books Henry ages three years, and McCloskey changes his haircut a bit, gives him height, and takes away some of the awkward gangliness of the first illustrations. Henry remains, though, extraordinarily skinny; Homer Price might have found him a bit anemic.

The title-page illustration has Henry waving out of the packed station wagon, inviting the reader into the book and establishing an intimate relationship with the reader; though the other characters share Henry's experiences, only the reader shares his journal.[10] This is stressed at the end of the novel, when the final illustration on the final page shows Henry sitting on his suitcase, looking back at the reader as he writes in his journal. The suggestion is that this journal has a very specific audience besides the writer himself.

In fact, a number of the illustrations stress Henry's keeping of a journal, something that does not appear in any of the other books. The illustration for the opening chapter shows Henry writing in his airplane seat, and the text explains the peculiar importance of this journal as opposed to the other three:

> I am going to keep this journal, and when the trip is over I'm going to edit it and publish it. When you look at my book you'll find what you want to know, not just the names of restaurants, motels and museums. It will tell what states sell firecrackers, where the best rodeos are held and when, where there's good fishing, what to use for bait, where the amusement parks are located, where you can get good root beer, and whether the natives of the different towns are friendly or hostile. (12)

So Henry writes within an airplane (9), by a pool (87), and while on a suitcase (220).

The sources of humor are slightly different in the second novel, though, like the first, they still depend a great deal on character pose and expression. One source is the family car which is packed tighter and tighter as the journey goes on, mostly because of additions by Henry and Midge. The first image of the car shows suitcases on top, but the inside nearly empty (48). Later Midge and Henry heave an enormous bag of pinecones onto the roof; the suitcases have gone inside (73). By the time they head back from Kansas, they have added a birdcage and are pulling a canvas-topped trailer (213).

Another source of humor is the dichotomy between very skinny characters like Henry and Midge, and the somewhat more rotund ones they encounter during their trip. Such encounters occur in San Francisco (34), Arizona (132), Denver (170), and Grover's Corner (216). In each case the larger character is opposed to the relatively diminutive Henry, and the contrast puts the larger character in the comic role.

Twice in the four novels McCloskey used a double-page spread for an illustration; in both cases the illustration extends to all the borders of the page. In *Henry Reed's Journey* McCloskey uses this spread to illustrate the cataclysm of the fireworks as the travelers arrive home (216–17). Henry and Midge gleefully watch from the car as all the fireworks explode, sending the gathered welcomers in all directions. McCloskey is a bit like Burt Dow here, painting wild shapes and designs to suggest the explosions. Since Henry had been writing about fireworks throughout the novel, Mc-Closkey's illustration comes as a fitting climax.

The only other double-page spread comes in the final book that McCloskey illustrated: *Henry Reed's Big Show.* Here he illus-trates music of the late 1960s by drawing jumbles and geomet-ric shapes, tangles of G-clefs and musical notations, random splotches, sunbursts, and abstract lines.[11] All of these are placed behind the four musicians and seem to funnel into the ears of a policeman standing nearby. The confusion, disorderliness, and random nature of the designs present an image that pleases some characters—notably Henry, Midge, and their friends—while dis-pleasing the adult world.

Though Henry has difficulty with the adult world in *Henry Reed's Big Show,* it is principally with the child world that he has difficulty in *Henry Reed's Baby-Sitting Service,* the third book in the series. In terms of plot chronology, this book begins directly after *Henry Reed's Journey*. It deals with Henry's new business—baby-sitting—and recounts the trials of that profession. Henry encounters children who assault him, who disappear, who lose the family trailer, who hear terrible screams and moans. He remains poised and calm through each episode.

The illustrations for this novel add nothing new to the series. The most innovative pictures are those of Belinda Osborn, who disappears on cue. She is the most comic child in the text and the most developed by Robertson; she also seems to be the most interesting for McCloskey. As in *Henry Reed, Inc.*, McCloskey pictures things in the way that Henry would see them. Belinda appears as a slightly askew character, with unnaturally large and penetrating eyes.[12] Another illustration in the chapter that introduces her shows Henry desperately searching; he looks down a corridor of seemingly endless doors, with infinite possibilities for hiding (79).

One other illustration is significant; it occurs between the title page and the beginning of the text. Henry is moving back into his bedroom at Grover's Corner. Holding onto a suit about to be put into the closet, he looks down happily at Agony, who sits in his open suitcase, wagging his tail and scattering the clothes. The picture works as a bridge between the novel and the previous one.

Four years later Viking published the final book in the Henry Reed series that McCloskey was to illustrate; it was also McCloskey's final collaborative work. *Henry Reed's Big Show* presents a slightly older Henry Reed, and it chronicles his attempts first to stage a play and then to stage a rodeo. When the actors abandon the first project, Henry organizes all the animals he has met in the book—including Midge's ungainly horse—into a rodeo that climaxes in a stampede. Henry concludes wanly that instead of becoming a theatrical producer, "I think I'll be a naturalist" (206).

McCloskey included fewer illustrations for this novel than any of the others, less than a third of what he had used in *Henry Reed, Inc.* The cover illustration is the most complex, though it does not illustrate something that actually happens in the novel. Henry stands surrounded by two diminutive knights (a remnant of the rodeo), Midge's horse Galileo (who dominates most of the adventures), two musicians from a group that puts on an impromptu show for Henry, and Midge, who looks up at him expectantly. Henry, wearing a top hat, is calm and in control of the chaos. In fact, this is his stance throughout the novel.

The proximity of Henry and Midge in this illustration is mirrored in later pictures. Henry and Midge are frequently paired alone; even in crowds they are grouped together as a couple who share perceptions and reactions. Over the course of the four novels Henry has moved from a grudging acceptance of her partnership to a position where he can state, "Midge Glass is my special friend and business partner" (9). It is this special friendship that McCloskey captures in many of his illustrations.

The Henry Reed series has remained popular over thirty years; all of the books in the series are still in print. Certainly one reason for their continued success is the unity of vision between author and illustrator. Though McCloskey's illustrations are not as innovative as those for *Trigger John's Son* and *Junket*, they match the text's description of a character more than in any other of his collaborative works. Henry Reed as defined by McCloskey matches Henry Reed as defined by Robertson, so that the two visions become inseparable.

Conclusion

The May Massee Collection kept by Emporia State University holds one of the many logbooks kept by May Massee's secretary, listing, in beautiful, regular handwriting, the reception of manuscripts and their eventual fate. Kept during the middle of the 1930s, it is a chronicle of May Massee's standards, for virtually every manuscript is marked as "returned." One is of particular interest; next to the proposed title is a familiar name in children's literature: Theodore Geisel (Dr. Seuss).[1] It too is marked "returned," and in fact, Dr. Seuss would never publish a book with May Massee or the Viking Press.

Perhaps commercially this was not a wise rejection, but the decision does suggest something about May Massee's approach to children's literature, and that is that children's literature must speak directly to and specifically of the child's perceived experience. The nonsense for the sake of nonsense of Dr. Seuss, delightful and imaginative as it is, is limited in its ability to deal with that perceived experience. Massee chose authors who wrote and drew what a child would immediately apprehend as being close to the world at hand.

The list of authors and illustrators that she gathered around her during the 1930s, 1940s, and 1950s suggests this vision. Ludwig Bemelmans captured the life of a young, mischievous girl living in Paris. Ingri and Paul Parin D'Aulaire shaped their biographies for the child by focusing on details a child would recognize as part of his or her own life. Astrid Lindgren played out some of the escapist fantasies that children contrive. James Daugherty, in a book such as *Andy and the Lion,* expressed the imaginative life of the child. Marie Hall Ets and Rachel Field quietly celebrated a child's inner life. Don Freeman, Munro Leaf, Kurt Wiese, and Robert Lawson created characters who had the

147

same need for a security, a home, and acceptance that all children have.

Certainly McCloskey had an affinity to some of Massee's earliest artists in terms of his style of illustration. He is closest to James Daugherty and Robert Lawson. All three share the bold use of line, the use of characters with extreme poses and exaggerated characteristics, the restriction of color, the combination of detail and white space to evoke complex settings. But all three shared Massee's understanding of children's literature as well, and the reader of these authors finds a similar concern with a child's use of the imagination to come to grips with the world. The child might be set in the guise of an animal (*Ferdinand, Rabbit Hill*). The child protagonist, rather than the author, might spin a fantasy (*Andy and the Lion*). Or the child protagonist might generate an inner fantasy set against a realistic landscape (*One Morning in Maine*). But in each case the child protagonist uses the imagination to order and understand.

And this is precisely why the advent of authors and illustrators who explored the psychological makeup of children—Maurice Sendak chief among them—spelled the end of the age of May Massee. Where McCloskey's characters—and Lawson's, Daugherty's, Munro Leaf's, and Ludwig Bemelmans's—used the imagination to order outside experience, those of Sendak used it to order inner psychological experience, experience that a child might not even consciously recognize. The result is that while McCloskey examines the child in the context of a family, drawing love and security from that family, Sendak examines the child outside of the family, using the imagination to look inward and escape the insecurity and loneliness that the absence of the family has generated. If McCloskey had illustrated Sendak's *Dear Mili* (1988) (this is hard to imagine), one suspects that in the final illustration the child would not be treading warily, warily towards the skeletal, outstretched arms of the old crone as the sun sinks into the valley in the background. There would be a grand confusion of sheer joy at reunion, perhaps a dog thumping its tail and shoving its muzzle into their midst, and a real sense that "home" had once again been established. This is not to denigrate

Sendak's vision; it is only to illustrate the wide gulf that emerged between children's literature before and after *Where the Wild Things Are.*

McCloskey's vision of children's literature is the more remarkable considering that the two decades of his career in children's literature spanned the most turbulent time of the twentieth century. *Lentil* was published as France had fallen, England seemed about to succumb, and Roosevelt was rushing supplies to shore up the allies. *Blueberries for Sal* was issued during the beginning of the cold war, and *One Morning in Maine* during the height of the Korean War. *Time of Wonder* came during one of the most intense periods of nuclear arms testing in the country's history, and *Burt Dow* came after the assassination of a president and during the move into Vietnam.

In the midst of this dreadful world—in the midst of folly and violence and threatened destruction—appeared a series of books that celebrated childhood, family, friendship, the natural world—in short, life itself. If this seems an anomaly, it might be noted that McCloskey's vision in his children's books is one of absolute affirmation of the permanence and beauty and significance of the world. "You snap off the light and row toward the dock as the stars are gazing down, their reflections gazing up," he writes in *Time of Wonder.* "In the quiet of the night one hundred pairs of eyes are watching you, while one pair of eyes is watching over all" (28). The numinous quality of this affirmation denies the despair that might be caused by a world at war.

To search for the significance of Robert McCloskey in children's literature one would not look at sheer output: six picture books and two collections of short stories is not a vast amount by the standards of many children's authors and illustrators of the 1980s. Nor would one look only at awards, though McCloskey's record of two Caldecott Medals and three Caldecott Honors for six works is unmatched. Nor would one look for disciples who copied his approaches to story and art.

Instead, one would look at the affirming vision of McCloskey's books; it is this that ultimately has led to his continued popularity. The worlds of the Midwest, Boston, and the Maine coast are benevolent, full of wonder, physically splendid. They are homes, with all that that word connotes: warmth and security, family relationships, innocent joys, the freedom for children to grow and relish the unalloyed splendors and mysteries of the world that lies close about them. McCloskey's strength was his ability to deny the primacy of a world that chose to war with itself. "Yes, that's true," he might say, "but come see this. It is ever so much more important." And the reader is drawn from sadness to joy, from despair to hope, from denial to affirmation.

For in McCloskey's work the ducklings are forever following the swan boats until they swim to their island nest. Sal and Jane are forever returning home to a bowl of clam chowder. Burt Dow is heading up the bay toward land. And the blue water sparkles all around, all around, and the blue water sparkles all around.

Notes and References

Preface

1. *Robert McCloskey,* dir. Morton Schindel, Weston Woods, 1964.
2. Quoted in Ethel Heins, "Bothering to Look: A Conversation Between Robert McCloskey and Ethel Heins," in Barbara Harrison and Gregory Maguire, eds., *Innocence and Experience: Essays and Conversations on Children's Literature* (New York: Lothrop, Lee, & Shepherd, 1987), 326–40. See also McCloskey's comments on perception in his "Caldecott Award Acceptance," *Horn Book* 34 (1958):245–51.
3. "The Creative Process: A May Massee Workshop" (Emporia, Kansas: Emporia State University, 20 June 1973), with Robert Burch, Carolyn Field, Margaret Lesser Foster, Doris Gates, Milton Glick, and Robert McCloskey.

Chapter One

1. May Massee, "American Institute of Graphic Arts Medal to May Massee: Acceptance," *Horn Book* 35 (August 1959):275–77.
2. *Robert McCloskey,* directed by Morton Schindel, Weston Woods, 1964.
3. Stuart Fitton, personal interview, 20 September 1988.
4. *McCloskey,* Weston Woods.
5. "Robert McCloskey" (New York: Viking Press, n.d.), unpaged.
6. Ibid. For comments on McCloskey's interest in inventions see Marc Simont, "Bob McCloskey, Inventor," *Horn Book* 34 (August 1958):256–57.
7. *McCloskey,* Weston Woods.
8. Ibid.
9. Personal interview, 20 August 1987.
10. "The May Massee Workshop on Oral History" (Emporia, Kansas: Emporia State University, 1 August 1983), with Robert McCloskey and Margaret McElderry.

11. "McCloskey," Viking Press.

12. "Oral History."

13. "McCloskey," Viking Press.

14. May Massee, interview by Morton Schindel, 1962. See George V. Hodowanec, ed., *The May Massee Collection: Creative Publishing for Children, 1923–1963: A Checklist* (Emporia, Kansas: Emporia State University, 1979), 280.

15. "The Creative Process."

16. "Oral History."

17. Ibid.

18. Ibid.

19. Heins, "Bothering to Look."

20. Ibid.

21. Ibid.

22. Cited in Ethel L. Heins, "From Mallards to Maine: A Conversation with Robert McCloskey," *Journal of Youth Services in Libraries* 1 (Winter 1988):187–93.

23. See Item 550 in *The May Massee Collection.*

24. May Massee, letter to Bertha Miller, 2 July 1943. See Item 550 and p. 282 in *The May Massee Collection.*

25. May Massee, letter to Bertha Miller, 23 September 1943. See Item 550 and p. 282 in *The May Massee Collection.*

26. May Massee, letter to Bertha Miller, 24 September 1943. See Item 550 and p. 282 in *The May Massee Collection.*

27. May Massee, letter to Bertha Miller, 11 October 1943. See Item 550 and p. 282 in *The May Massee Collection.*

28. James Daugherty and Eric Gugler, "*Homer Price* [Comment by Eric Gugler and James Daugherty]," *Horn Book* 19 (November 1943):424–26.

29. Ibid.

30. See the reprint of this letter in *The May Massee Collection,* 138–39.

31. Cited in Margaret McCloskey, "Robert McCloskey," *Horn Book* 34 (August 1958):252–55.

32. See Item 550 in *The May Massee Collection.*

33. Ruth Sawyer, letter to Jessie Orton Jones and Elizabeth Orton Jones, October 1943. Though not listed in *The May Massee Collection,* this letter is housed in the collection at Emporia State University.

34. Cited in Edgar Allen Beem, "'Kuplink, Kuplank, Kuplunk!' A Brief Glimpse into Robert McCloskey's Picture-Book World of Childhood and Summertime in Maine," *Maine Times,* 7 August 1987, 20–23.

35. "Oral History."

36. McCloskey, personal interview.

37. Heins, "Bothering to Look," 326–40.

38. *Lentil* (New York: Viking Press, 1940), unpaged.

Chapter Two

1. Personal interview, 20 August 1987.

2. *Lentil* (New York: Viking Press, 1940), unpaged. All further references to this text are from this edition.

3. Personal interview, 20 August 1987.

4. Personal interview, 20 August 1987.

5. *McCloskey*, Weston Woods.

6. Anne T. Eaton, review of *Lentil, New York Times Book Review*, 19 May 1940, 10.

7. "The Creative Process."

8. McCloskey himself was not pleased with the final result of the lithograph drawing of Lentil and his harmonica, and changed it somewhat when Weston Woods filmed *Lentil* iconographically in 1956. Personal letter to the author, 20 September 1988.

9. Review of *Homer Price, Saturday Review* 26 (16 October 1943):60.

10. "Oral History."

11. *McCloskey*, Weston Woods.

12. Daugherty and Gugler, "*Homer Price*," 424–26.

13. See the reprint of this letter in *The May Massee Collection*, 138–39.

14. Review of *Homer Price, Saturday Review* 26 (16 October 1943):60.

15. Linda Silver, "Ohio Boyhoods: A Study of Adolescence in Novels by Robert McCloskey, Virginia Hamilton, and Don Moser," *Mid-America: The Yearbook of the Society for the Study of Midwestern Literature* 9 (1982):114–23.

16. *Homer Price* (New York: Viking Press, 1943), 134. Hereafter page references cited parenthetically in the text.

17. Personal interview, 20 April 1987.

18. Personal interview, 20 August 1987.

19. "Caldecott Award Acceptance," *Horn Book* 34 (August 1958):245–51.

20. See Item 549 in *The May Massee Collection*.

21. *Centerburg Tales* (New York: Viking Press, 1951), 11. Hereafter page references cited parenthetically in the text.

22. See Item 549 in *The May Massee Collection*.

23. *McCloskey*, Weston Woods.

24. See Item 549 in *The May Massee Collection*.

Chapter Three

1. Anne Malcolmson, *Yankee Doodle's Cousins* (Boston: Houghton Mifflin Co., 1941), vii. Hereafter page references cited parenthetically in the text.
2. Personal interview, 20 August 1987.
3. Alice Jordan, review of *Yankee Doodle's Cousins*, *Horn Book* 17 (November 1941):473.
4. Ellen Lewis Buell, review of *Yankee Doodle's Cousins, New York Times Book Review,* 4 January 1942, 9.
5. Robert H. Davis, *Tree Toad* (Philadelphia: J. P. Lippincott, 1942), xv. Hereafter page references cited parenthetically in the text.
6. Personal interview, 20 August 1987.
7. Claire Huchet Bishop, *The Man Who Lost His Head* (New York: Viking Press, 1942), unpaged. All further references to this text are from this edition.
8. See Item 105 in *The May Massee Collection.*
9. Personal interview, 20 August 1987.
10. *Horn Book* 25 (September 1949):401, 426.
11. Ibid., 426.
12. Anne Carroll Moore, review of *Trigger John's Son, Horn Book* 25 (November 1949):522.
13. Robert McCloskey, letter to the author, 20 September 1988.
14. Thomas Pendleton Robinson, *Trigger John's Son* (New York: Viking Press, 1949). All further references to this text are from this edition.

Chapter Four

1. "Caldecott Award Acceptance Speech," *Horn Book* 18 (August 1942):277–82.
2. *McCloskey,* Weston Woods.
3. "The Creative Process."
4. Cited in Heins, "Bothering to Look," 326–40.
5. Marc Simont, letter to the author, 21 March 1988.
6. Robert McCloskey, *Make Way for Ducklings* (New York: Viking Press, 1941), unpaged. All further references to this text are from this edition.
7. "Caldecott Acceptance," *Horn Book,* August 1942.
8. The original dummy for *Make Way for Ducklings* is preserved in the May Massee Collection of Emporia State University, Emporia, Kansas. See Item 552 in *The May Massee Collection.*
9. Helen W. Painter, "Robert McCloskey: Master of Humorous Realism," *Elementary English* 45 (February 1968):145–58.

10. Nancy Larrick, "Robert McCloskey's *Make Way for Ducklings*," *Elementary English* 37 (March 1960):143–48.

11. Ibid.

12. "Caldecott Acceptance," 1942.

13. "Ducklings at Home and Abroad," in Bertha M. Miller and Elinor W. Field, eds., *Caldecott Medal Books: 1938–1957* (Boston: The Horn Book, 1957), 79–84. Cited in Painter, "Master of Humorous Realism."

14. Larrick, "Robert McCloskey."

15. McCloskey, "The Creative Process."

16. "Caldecott Acceptance," 1942.

17. Marc Simont, letter to the author, 21 March 1988.

18. "Caldecott Acceptance," 1942.

19. "Oral History."

20. See Item 552 in *The May Massee Collection*

21. "Oral History." See Item 552 in *The May Massee Collection*.

22. Alice Jordan, review of *Make Way for Ducklings, Horn Book* 17 (September 1941):359.

23. Ellen Lewis Buell, review of *Make Way for Ducklings, New York Times Book Review,* 19 October 1941, 10.

24. Warren Chappell, review of *Make Way for Ducklings, Horn Book* 17 (September 1941):450.

25. Review of *Make Way for Ducklings, New Yorker* 17 (6 December 1941):110–11.

26. Anne Carroll Moore, review of *Make Way for Ducklings, Horn Book* 17 (September 1941):381.

27. Personal interview, 20 August 1987.

28. *McCloskey,* Weston Woods.

29. "Caldecott Acceptance," 1942.

30. May Massee, letter to Pauline Bloom, 31 October 1951. See Item 552 and p. 281 in *The May Massee Collection*.

31. "Caldecott Acceptance," 1942.

Chapter Five

1. Anne Carroll Moore, "The Three Owls' Notebook," *Horn Book* 24 (November 1948):434–36.

2. Personal interview, 20 August 1987.

3. *Blueberries for Sal* (New York: Viking Press, 1948), 38. Hereafter page references cited parenthetically in the text.

4. See Item 547 in *The May Massee Collection*.

5. In two illustrations cut from the original dummy, the two mothers do meet. When both recognize that the noise behind them is not com-

ing from their own child, they slowly back up and up the hill until they back into each other on the summit. Startled, they turn around, reverse positions, and rush down the other sides of the hill where they find their appropriate child. Aside from the thematic difficulty of having the mothers meet, these drawings have an air of caricature about them that is quite different from the stance of the rest of the book. See Item 547 in *The May Massee Collection.*

6. "The Creative Process."

7. See Item 547 in *The May Massee Collection.*

8. The original pen-and-ink drawing for the endpapers to *Blueberries for Sal* is now housed in the Special Children's Collection of the Free Library of Philadelphia.

9. Myriam Wilson, review of *Blueberries for Sal, New Republic* 119 (6 December 1948):32.

10. See Item 547 in *The May Massee Collection,* which includes the sketchbooks for *Blueberries for Sal.* McCloskey brought these same sketchbooks to Italy, where he drew landscapes and a cart and horse at an open market in 1949. The *National Geographic* articles he used in preparing the drawings for *Blueberries for Sal* were: Frederick V. Coville, "The Wild Blueberry Tamed: The New Industry of the Pine Barrens of New Jersey," *National Geographic Magazine* 29 (June 1916):535–46; "American Berries of Hill, Dale, and Wayside," *National Geographic Magazine* 35 (February 1919):168–84. This anonymous article included colored plates of drawings by Mary E. Eaton.

11. *One Morning in Maine* (New York: Viking Press, 1952), 6. Hereafter page references cited parenthetically in the text.

12. See Item 553 in *The May Massee Collection.*

13. Though Marcia Brown, Leo and Diane Dillon, and Barbara Cooney have each won two Caldecott Awards, only one other illustrator has won two awards for books both written and illustrated by himself: Chris Van Allsburg, for *Jumanji* (1982) and *The Polar Express* (1986).

14. "Caldecott Award Acceptance," *Horn Book* 34 (1958):245–51.

15. Ibid.

16. *Homer Price,* 140.

17. "Caldecott Acceptance," 1958.

18. *Time of Wonder* (New York: Viking Press, 1957), 62. Hereafter page references cited parenthetically in the text.

19. "Caldecott Acceptance," 1958.

20. Morris Colman, letter to Robert McCloskey, 2 August 1957. See p. 288 in *The May Massee Collection.*

21. Heins, "From Mallards to Maine."

22. Frances Lander Spain, review of *Time of Wonder, Saturday Review* 40 (21 December 1957):38.

23. Ellen Lewis Buell, review of *Time of Wonder, New York Times Book Review,* 2 February 1958, 28.
24. Jennie D. Lindquist, review of *Time of Wonder, Horn Book* 33 (December 1957):480.
25. Cited in Beem, "'Kuplink, Kuplank, Kuplunk!'"
26. *Burt Dow: Deep-Water Man* (New York: Viking Press, 7. Hereafter page references cited parenthetically in the text.
27. See Item 548 in *The May Massee Collection.*
28. See McCloskey's discussion of this in Heins, "Bothering to Look," 326–40.
29. "Creative Process."
31. *McCloskey,* Weston Woods.
32. Personal interview, 20 August 1987.
33. See Item 548 in *The May Massee Collection.* Massee shared McCloskey's skepticism about books with a controlled vocabulary. See May Massee, "Publishing Children's Books Today," *Horn Book* 25 (September 1949):396–400.
34. Heins, "Bothering to Look."

Chapter Six

1. Ruth Sawyer, *Journey Cake Ho!* (New York: Viking Press, 1953), 26. Hereafter page references cited parenthetically in the text.
2. Anne H. White, *Junket, The Dog Who Liked Everything "Just So"* (New York: Viking Press, 1955). Hereafter page references cited parenthetically in the text.
3. Frances Lander Spain, review of *Junket, Saturday Review* 38 (19 March 1955):40.
4. Marjorie Fisher, review of *Junket, New York Times Book Review,* 19 June 1955, 18.
5. Katherine Kinkead, review of *Junket, New Yorker* 31 (26 November 1955):223.
6. Personal interview, 20 August 1987.
7. Keith Robertson, letter to the author, 13 July 1987.
8. Personal interview, 20 August 1987.
9. Keith Robertson, *Henry Reed, Inc.* (New York: Viking Press, 1958), 26. Hereafter page references cited parenthetically in the text.
10. Keith Robertson, *Henry Reed's Journey* (New York: Viking Press, 1963). Hereafter page references cited parenthetically in the text.
11. Keith Robertson, *Henry Reed's Big Show* (New York: Viking Press, 1970, 66–67. All further references to this text are from this edition.

12. Keith Robertson, *Henry Reed's Baby-Sitting Service* (New York: Viking Press, 1966), 81. Hereafter page references cited parenthetically in the text.

Conclusion

1. See *The May Massee Collection*, 313.

Selected Bibliography

Primary Works

Works Written and Illustrated

Blueberries for Sal. New York: Viking Press, 1948.
Burt Dow: Deep-Water Man. New York: Viking Press, 1963.
Centerburg Tales. New York: Viking Press, 1951.
Homer Price. New York: Viking Press, 1943.
Lentil. New York: Viking Press, 1940.
Make Way for Ducklings. New York: Viking Press, 1941.
One Morning in Maine. New York: Viking Press, 1952.
Time of Wonder. New York: Viking Press, 1957.

Works Illustrated

American History Club. *George Washington Bicentennial Calendar.* Hamilton, Ohio: American History Club of Hamilton High School, 1932.
Bishop, Claire Huchet. *The Man Who Lost His Head.* New York: Viking Press, 1942.
Davis, Robert H. *Tree Toad.* Philadelphia: J. P. Lippincott, 1942.
Malcolmson, Anne. *Yankee Doodle's Cousins.* Boston: Houghton Mifflin, 1941.
Robertson, Keith. *Henry Reed, Inc.* New York: Viking Press, 1958.
———. *Henry Reed's Baby-Sitting Service.* New York: Viking Press, 1966.
———. *Henry Reed's Big Show.* New York: Viking Press, 1970.
———. *Henry Reed's Journey.* New York: Viking Press, 1963.
Robinson, Thomas Pendleton. *Trigger John's Son.* New York: Viking Press, 1949.
Sawyer, Ruth. *Journey Cake, Ho!* New York: Viking Press, 1953.
White, Anne H. *Junket, the Dog Who Liked Everything "Just So."* New York: Viking Press, 1955.

Writings on Children's Literature

"Caldecott Award Acceptance." *Horn Book* 18 (August 1942):277–82. Reprinted as "Ducklings at Home and Abroad." In *Caldecott Medal Books: 1938–1957,* edited by Bertha M. Miller and Elinor W. Field, 79–84. Boston: The Horn Book, 1957.

"Caldecott Award Acceptance." *Horn Book* 34 (August 1958):245–51. Reprinted in *Newbery and Caldecott Medal Books: 1956–1965,* edited by Lee Kingman, 188–93. Boston: The Horn Book, 1965.

"Peeping." In *Vistas in Reading. Proceedings of the International Reading Association, 1966,* edited by J. Allen Figurel, vol. 11, part 1, 21–24. Newark, Del.: International Reading Association, 1967.

"Robert McCloskey." In *The Junior Book of Authors,* edited by Stanley J. Kunitz and Howard Haycraft, 2d rev. ed., 203–4. New York: H. W. Wilson Co., 1951.

Secondary Works

Biographical Studies

Beem, Edgar Allen. "'Kuplink, Kuplank, Kuplunk!' A Brief Glimpse into Robert McCloskey's Picture-Book World of Childhood and Summer in Maine." *Maine Times,* 7 August 1987, 20–23. Discusses *Blueberries for Sal, One Morning in Maine,* and *Time of Wonder* in the context of McCloskey's biography, focusing principally on the experience of living in Maine.

Hopkins, Lee Bennett. "Robert McCloskey." In *Books Are By People.* New York: Citation Press, 1969, 164–68. Examines *Lentil* and *Homer Price* in the context of McCloskey's biography.

Massee, May. "Robert McCloskey—Wins Second Caldecott Medal." *Library Journal* 83 (15 April 1958):1243–44, 1248. Recounts McCloskey's life and work from the period between *Lentil* and *Time of Wonder.*

McCloskey, Margaret. "Robert McCloskey." *Horn Book* 34 (August 1958):252–55. Reprinted as "Robert McCloskey—Biographical Note." In *Newbery and Caldecott Medal Books: 1956–1965,* edited by Lee Kingman, 194–95. Boston: The Horn Book, 1965. Briefly examines McCloskey's family life and work in children's literature until 1957.

"Robert McCloskey." New York: Viking Press, n.d. Short promotional pamphlet including some comments by McCloskey on his early life. Recounts a brief outline of his career by focusing on the published works.

Simont, Marc. "Bob McCloskey, Inventor." *Horn Book* 34 (August

1958):256–57. Reprinted in *Newbery and Caldecott Medal Books: 1956–65,* edited by Lee Kingman, 196–97. Boston: The Horn Book, 1965. Recalls McCloskey's love of machinery, focusing on the needs associated with living on an island.

Interviews and Colloquia

"'Bothering to Look': A Conversation Between Robert McCloskey and Ethel Heins." In *Innocence and Experience: Essays and Conversations on Children's Literature,* edited by Barbara Harrison and Gregory Maguire, 326–40. New York: Lothrop, Lee & Shepherd Books, 1987.

"The Creative Process: A May Massee Workshop." Emporia, Kansas: Emporia State University, 20 June 1973. With Robert Burch, Carolyn Field, Margaret Lesser Foster, Doris Gates, Milton Glick, and Robert McCloskey. Unpublished.

"From Mallards to Maine: A Conversation with Robert McCloskey." [Interview by Ethel L. Heins.] *Journal of Youth Services in Libraries* 1 (Winter 1988):187–93.

"The May Massee Workshop on Oral History." Emporia, Kansas: Emporia State University, 1 August 1983. With Robert McCloskey and Margaret McElderry. Unpublished.

Critical Studies

Archer, Marguerite P. "Robert McCloskey, Student of Human Nature." *Elementary English* 35 (May 1958):287–96. Examines motifs in McCloskey's Ohio books that have connections to his biography.

Daugherty, James, and Eric Gugler. "*Homer Price* [Comment by Eric Gugler and James Daugherty]." *Horn Book* 19 (November 1943):424–26. Two comments dealing with the genre and artistry of *Homer Price.* Suggests that *Homer Price* is of the same genre as *Tom Sawyer* and participates in a celebration of American values.

Harbage, Mary. "Robert McCloskey, He Doesn't Forget." *Elementary English* 31 (May 1954):251–59. Argues that McCloskey's humor generates from his own memories of growing up in the Midwest.

Larrick, Nancy. "Robert McCloskey's *Make Way for Ducklings.*" *Elementary English* 37 (March 1960):143–48. A close account of how *Make Way for Ducklings* moved from idea to finished book, dealing also with the actual production process. Concludes with comments on the nature of drawing and the importance of "seeing" the natural world.

Manna, Anthony L. "Robert McCloskey's *Make Way for Ducklings:* The Art of Regional Storytelling." In *Touchstones: Reflections on the Best in Children's Literature,* vol. 3, edited by Perry Nodelman, 90–100. West Lafayette, Ind.: Children's Literature Association Publishers, 1989. A survey of McCloskey's picture books and Homer Price books. Argues that the books are regional in terms of their concerns.

Painter, Helen. "Robert McCloskey: Master of Humorous Realism." *Elementary English* 45 (February 1968):145–58. Reprinted in *Authors and Illustrators of Children's Books,* edited by Miriam Hoffman and Eva Samuels, 308–26. New York: Bowker, 1972. Touches briefly on all the books that McCloskey both wrote and illustrated, connecting them to his biography. Asserts that the books represent the genre of humorous realism, where everyday events take on comic proportions.

Sawyer, Ruth. "Robert McCloskey: Good Craftsman and Fine Artist." *Publishers' Weekly* 141 (27 June 1942):2348–50. Focuses on McCloskey's artistry and ability to craft a tale. Asserts that his work is informed by a "shy gentleness."

Silver, Linda R. "Ohio Boyhoods: A Study of Adolescence in Novels by Robert McCloskey, Virginia Hamilton, and Don Moser." *Mid-America: The Yearbook of the Society for the Study of Midwestern Literature* 9 (1982):114–23. Asserts that Homer Price is actually an adolescent, and the book should be read geographically. Centerburg is archetypal in that it paints an innocent, perhaps naive world whose people share "a common purpose, common values, and a firm faith in the future."

Film

Schindel, Morton, dir. *Robert McCloskey.* Weston Woods, 1964. Presents biographical material, focusing primarily on McCloskey's life on the islands of Penobscot Bay. Examines the movement from idea, to text, to illustrations, to finished book by using *Burt Dow* as the principal example. Narrated by McCloskey.

Catalog

Hodowanec, George V., ed. *The May Massee Collection: Creative Publishing for Children, 1923–1963: A Checklist.* Emporia, Kansas: Emporia State University, 1979. A catalog listing each item in the May Massee Collection, including much of McCloskey's original work.

Index

About the Author

Gary D. Schmidt received his B.A. from Gordon College, Wenham, Massachusetts, and his M.A. and Ph.D. in medieval literature from the University of Illinois at Urbana-Champaign. An associate professor of English at Calvin College, Grand Rapids, Michigan, he teaches children's literature, medieval and renaissance literature, and the history of the English language. He is especially interested in the role of the narrator, and has coedited a collection of essays, *The Voice of the Narrator in Children's Literature,* published by Greenwood Press. The author of articles in *Children's Literature in Education,* the *Children's Literature Association Quarterly, Mediaevalia,* and the *Journal of the Rocky Mountain Medieval and Renaissance Association,* he is currently editing the twelfth-century *Vision of the Monk of Evesham* and writing a study about Hugh Lofting, the creator of Dr. Dolittle.